15 days

of prayer with

BROTHER ROGER OF TAIZÉ

15 days
of prayer series

On a journey, it's good to have a guide. Even great saints took spiritual directors or confessors with them on their itineraries toward sanctity. Now you can be guided by the most influential spiritual figures of all time. The 15 Days of Prayer series introduces their deepest and most personal thoughts.

This popular series is perfect if you are looking for a gift, or if you want to be introduced to a particular guide and his or her spirituality. Each volume contains:

- ⋄ A brief biography of the saint or spiritual leader
- ⋄ A guide to creating a format for prayer or retreat
- ⋄ Fifteen meditation sessions with focus points and reflection guides

15 days
of prayer with
BROTHER ROGER OF TAIZÉ

Sabine Laplane

TRANSLATED BY
JUDITH BRUDER

NEW CITY PRESS
Hyde Park, NY

Published in the United States by New City Press
202 Comforter Blvd., Hyde Park, NY 12538
www.newcitypress.com
©2010 New City Press (English translation)

This book is a translation of *Prier 15 Jours avec Frère Roger de Taizé*,
published by Nouvelle Cité, 2008,
Domaine d'Arny, 91680 Bruyères-le-Châtel.

All scores reproduced at the end of each chapter and all quotations
from Brother Roger are
© Ateliers et Presses de Taizé, 71250 Taizé, France

Cover design by Durva Correia

Library of Congress Cataloging-in-Publication Data:

A copy of the CIP data is available from the Library of Congress.
ISBN: 978-1-56548-349-1

Printed in the United States of America

Contents

How to Use This Book

*L*ike the others in this series, this book is an invitation to spend some time in the company of someone who can become, for a while, like a companion on our journey of prayer — someone who can help us draw inspiration from the sources that gave astonishing vitality to his own life.

Brother Roger cannot be taken as an isolated, individual spiritual figure: his life is inseparable from the existence of the Taizé Community in France. He founded the Community in solitude at the age of twenty-five at the height of the Second World War, and remained its leader as it grew for sixty-five years until at the age of ninety, in 2005, he was fatally attacked by a mentally disturbed assailant during evening prayers at Taizé.

The Taizé Community is now best known in the English-speaking world for its songs, which are very widely used in churches of all denominations. But the songs spring from the life of the Community, an ecumenical group of brothers living a modern form of monastic vocation, which welcomes tens of thousands of young adult pilgrims every year. And the Community came into existence, and became a beacon for so many people, largely through the vision of one man, Brother Roger.

So this book is an opportunity to get to know and to pray with a figure who touched countless thousands of lives and helped (in the words of Rowan Williams, Archbishop of Canterbury) change the whole climate of a religious culture.

Brother Roger was certainly a man of prayer, but that should not intimidate anyone. He never saw himself as a spiritual master, and never proposed methods or techniques of prayer or meditation that need to be studied and learned. He sought to be above all someone who listened. For him, trust in God was an entirely simple reality, so simple as to be accessible to everyone, and the same was true of prayer. He was well aware of the difficulties and even the reluctance that we can have to pray.

So this book does not present a program or ready-made itinerary of prayer. It points towards the insights that were at the heart of Brother Roger's life of prayer and of action, telling the story of the Taizé Community along the way.

Each of the fifteen chapters is followed by questions for reflection, to help the reader connect with these insights and perhaps make some of them his or her own. The book can, of course, be read straight through, but it is best if possible to give each chapter plenty of time. The chapters can accompany the stages of a quiet retreat, for those who have the opportunity. Or they can be read day by day, or week by week, during the course of everyday life. If there is an opportunity to give them quality time, in a place where you know you will not be disturbed, so much the better. Take time for the questions, too, to make links to the realities of your own life.

It can also be a good idea to underline, or to copy out, or to memorize a few of the words or phrases that you find most significant, so as to be able to come back to them again and again, to digest them, to let them hang around in the background during the day. (Brother Roger himself never hesitated to underline — in thick red felt pen — the phrases he found most important in his own favorite books!) What is important in these pages is not to take in everything, but what you can make your own, what helps open up for you the way towards God, source of Life.

The Editor

"And you, are you going to be someone who will open up the ways of trust in God?"

Brother Roger

Abbreviations

CH	*Choose to Love: Brother Roger of Taizé 1915–2005,* 2006
KS	Spink, Kathryn. *A Universal Heart: The Life and Vision of Brother Roger of Taizé,* 1986
UL	*Unfinished Letter* (Letter 2005)
GH	*Glimmers of Happiness,* 2007
PSH	*Praying in Silence of Heart,* 2007
L2004	*To the Sources of Joy* (Letter 2004)
PH	*Peace of Heart in All Things,* 2004
ST	*The Sources of Taizé,* 2000
GLA	*God is Love Alone,* 2003
L2000	*Astonished by Joy* (Letter 2000)
SHG	*Prayer: Seeking the Heart of God,* 1992
LF	*His Love is a Fire,* 1990
HT	*A Heart that Trusts,* 1986
DSF	*And Your Deserts Shall Flower,* 1984
WL	*The Wonder of a Love,* 1981

LND *A Life We Never Dared Hope For,* 1981

SC *Struggle and Contemplation,* 1974

F *Festival,* 1973

VP *Violent for Peace,* 1970

UP *Unanimity in Pluralism (Unanimité dans le pluralisme,* 1966*)*

DP *The Dynamic of the Provisional,* 1981

LTG *Living Today for God,* 1972

EN *Explanatory Notes (Communauté de Cluny, notes explicatives,* 1941*)*

Unless otherwise indicated, all chapter titles and subheads are quotations from Brother Roger.

Chronology of Brother Roger's Life

1915   Born on May 12th, in French-speaking Switzerland, the ninth child of Charles Schutz and his wife, Amélie Marsauche.

1931   Contracts tuberculosis. This illness will last for several years; for a time he will be in danger of death.

1936   Following his father's wishes, begins to study theology in Lausanne and Strasbourg.

1940   Chooses to leave neutral Switzerland and go to France, which is divided in half by the advance of the German troops, with the desire to bring a community into being. On August 20th he finds the village of Taizé, in Burgundy, close to the line of demarcation. He buys an old house and begins to offer hospitality to political refugees, mainly Jews.

1942 While visiting Geneva, learns that the occupation police has found out about him and that he cannot return to Taizé. Begins a community life in Geneva with the first three brothers. They return to Taizé in 1944.

1949 Seven brothers make a life-commitment to a common life lived in great simplicity. Brother Roger is prior. At the suggestion of Cardinal Gerlier of Lyons, he goes to Rome for the first time and has an audience with Pope Pius XII.

1951 Now that there are twelve brothers, some are sent to share the life of the poorest in different parts of the world. Later, Brother Roger will spend a few weeks each year in a place of poverty or division outside Europe; he will be in Chile after the coup d'état, in Lebanon during the war there, in South Africa, Calcutta …

1953 At Easter presents the "Rule of Taizé," expressing the essential aspects of the life of the growing community.

1958 First meeting with Pope John XXIII, who will become a point of reference for the community. From this time on, Brother Roger has audiences with the popes once a year.

1961 Brother Roger invites Catholic bishops and Protestant ministers to Taizé for three days. It is one of the first meetings of this sort since the Reformation in the sixteenth century.

1962 Visit to Constantinople to see the Orthodox Patriarch Athenagoras, whom he will meet on several occasions. On the way back, first visit to Eastern Europe (Bulgaria and Yugoslavia); later on he will return there several times (Poland, East Germany, Hungary, Czechoslovakia, Russia, Romania) until the fall of the Berlin Wall. Brother Roger is invited to participate in the Second Vatican Council as an observer. Together with Brother Max, he will take part in all the sessions of the Council until its closing in 1965.

1963 Takes part in the millennium celebrations of Mount Athos.

1966 First international meeting of young adults organized in Taizé. For several years, young people had been coming to Taizé spontaneously in ever growing numbers.

1974 Goes to London to receive the Templeton Prize for the progress of religion; in Frankfurt receives the German Peace Prize. Opening a "Council of Youth" in

Taizé, he writes his first open letter to young people.

1976 Mother Teresa of Calcutta makes her first visit to Taizé; in the same year he goes to Calcutta together with some brothers.

1978 First visit to Russia. In Paris, the first "European Meeting" of young adults is organized by the Taizé Community.

1985 Accompanied by children from every continent, brings to the Secretary-General of the United Nations, Javier Pérez de Cuellar, the suggestions of the young on how the UN can create trust between peoples. The same year, goes to Madras (India) for the first intercontinental meeting prepared by the Taizé Community in the Southern hemisphere.

1986 Pope John Paul II visits Taizé.

1988 Takes part in Moscow in the celebrations for the millennium of Christianity in Russia. The same year, receives the UNESCO prize for peace education.

1989 First young adult European meeting organized by the Taizé Community in Eastern Europe, in Wroclaw, Poland.

1992 The Archbishop of Canterbury, Dr. George Carey, spends a week in Taizé in the company of a thousand young Anglicans.

1995   Goes to Johannesburg, South Africa, for an international meeting of young Africans organized by the Taizé Community.

2004   Brother Roger's last young adult European Meeting, the 27th, in Lisbon.

2005   April 8, his last journey: to the funeral of Pope John Paul II in Rome.

August 16, attacked by a mentally disturbed assailant during evening prayer in the Church of Reconciliation in Taizé, and dies at the age of ninety. He is succeeded as Prior of Taizé by Brother Alois.

Brother Roger
of Taizé
(1915–2005)

*O*ur final glimpse of Brother Roger is of an old man so frail that he must always be accompanied. With faltering steps he moves slowly toward his usual place in the church, seated behind his brothers whom, at the age of 90, he still regards as his responsibility. Children cluster reassuringly around him. He seems so vulnerable, his voice no more than a thread; but there he is faithfully at evening prayer when death surprises him and stamps his life with a martyr's seal on August 16, 2005, just as hundreds of thousands of young adults are gathering in Cologne, Germany, for World Youth Day.

Through the Eyes of a Child

But let us begin this adventure at its beginning.

Roger Schutz-Marsauche was born on May 12th in the village of Provence in French-speaking

Switzerland. The youngest of a family of nine children, he led a sheltered childhood. His education was rigorous, marked by the strong discipline of an authoritarian father, but also by a kindhearted mother whose love of music instilled in him the joy of life.

He was an extremely sensitive child. As a teenager he was stricken by pulmonary tuberculosis and forced to spend long periods of time alone. A relapse even confronted him with the possibility of his own death. The idea of becoming a writer appealed to him, but his father did not consider this a suitable profession and insisted that he study theology at Lausanne. Later at Strasbourg he followed in his father's footsteps and became a pastor. But he was not in fact like his father. Young Roger felt himself called to something else.

To follow Christ with the gift of his whole life he trusted in something which his child's eye had glimpsed in his beloved and admired grandmother: that it is within oneself that one begins the process of reconciliation. It was from this woman, who had herself experienced the horrors of the First World War, that he inherited the conviction that peace in Europe would necessarily entail the reconciliation of Christians among themselves. A photograph of her in Brother Roger's room at Taizé shows her powerful determined gaze. Without being aware of it, she had opened a way forward for him. From her own devotion to Christ, she had spontaneously lived

out a wholly original ecumenism, that of a reconciliation which did not demand the repudia-
tion of anyone's spiritual family of origin from
whom they had acquired faith in the One Christ.
Rather, it allowed movement forward on a road
to mutual understanding.

"Love, and Say it with Your Life"
(St. Augustine)

Following his vision of a monastic community working for the unity of the Church, something unheard-of in Protestantism at that time,
Brother Roger came alone to Taizé in the early
1940's. The miseries around him soon moved
him to action. During the war, he hid Jewish
refugees from the Nazis. With the liberation, the
fledgling community began to concern itself with
German prisoners-of-war in two nearby camps.
And then there were all the young orphans who
needed a home and an education. What about
them? Brother Roger asked his sister Genevieve
to come and settle in the village and serve as a
"mother" to them. Later still, families uprooted
by wars around the globe — in Vietnam, Bosnia,
Rwanda — would be welcomed at Taizé. All
this in the name of the Gospel.

Brother Roger had taken for his own the direc-
tive of St. Augustine, which he liked to translate as
"Love, and say it with your life." Indeed, all suffering awoke in him an immediate and unqualified
response. "Something must be done," he could be

heard repeating, again and again. Once involved, his efforts were astonishing. Underlying his profound connection with Mother Teresa was their sharing of the same loving anxiety. Long before its formulation in the Second Vatican Council, he understood that "Christ is in some way united to every human being." His response? To live "a parable of communion." A few companions joined him, and so began the history of the Taizé Community. Unconfined by borders, small groups of brothers began to settle around the world in places of great poverty. Today there are more than 100 brothers. They come from all the continents and represent many different Christian denominations, each one committed by a "yes" for their whole life.

Taizé, That Little Springtime
(Pope John XXIII)

From the very beginning of its foundation, young people were attracted to Taizé. Even if it was not entirely finished with totalitarianism and ideologies, Western Europe was rebuilding and reforming itself with amazing dynamism. The Church was seeking new aspects of itself more open to the contemporary postwar world. An urgency of Christian witness was felt in a world scarred by memories and faced with the temptations of agnosticism, indifference, and materialism. And then, unexpectedly, Pope John XXIII announced the Second Vatican Council. He invited Brother Roger and Brother Max to attend as observers. The Taizé Community became better known. A French and German work-team built a church more spacious than the small Romanesque parish church and young people flooded in, bringing their urgent questions.

At first the brothers tried to preserve a monastic balance by preparing a place of welcome several miles away. But the imperative of Gospel hospitality demanded still greater efforts. God was knocking at the door. They must advance boldly, in the Holy Spirit. So ways were found to prepare the welcome at Taizé itself, to share that space of inner freedom which is common prayer, with its long silences. And, maybe, they could do even more. In that spirit, in 1971, the brothers went so far as to break down the walls of the recently completed Church of Reconciliation, and to install at the entrance an adjoining tent to further enlarge the space.... This highly symbolic action was the first of many such steps.

It also became necessary to simplify the liturgy, which became the opportunity to rediscover a traditional simple and repetitive prayer, similar to the Jesus Prayer so beloved of Eastern Christian spirituality. New kinds of chants, canons or simple invocations, grew out of a collaboration between the brothers and composers like Jacques Berthier. Some brothers themselves began to compose chants. This renewal began with Latin, but expanded to include more and more languages from every continent. These chants are now known worldwide. They can sustain this prayer of fifteen days as they sustained the prayer of Brother Roger. They can be found and learned on the Taizé website.

A Universal Heart

In an era of globalization, how could the brothers respond to the questions of pilgrims who came to this hill in Burgundy, and send them back to become involved in their local churches, without also taking into account the greater reality of the Church in the largest cities of Europe or on other continents? In nourishing itself on the Gospels the heart expands, and begins to beat in unison with the whole world. Once the challenge was understood as "living today for God," it sparked the creativity of Brother Roger and his brothers. Today vast meetings are organized from time to time on each continent, while other meetings take place regularly in different European cities.

Along with kindheartedness, simplicity does not exclude a search for beauty nor for a way of harmony which reveals something to us about the tenderness of our God: relying on the generosity of God's gift in each person; listening, rather than giving advice; living in wonder, and letting our hearts thrill. This, then, is Brother Roger's invitation to us: "*to try and understand another human being fully.*" What is essential in interpersonal relationships is equally essential for relationships among churches. Pope John XXIII's warm welcome had moved Brother Roger so deeply that it was decisive in his understanding of the ministry of communion of the Bishop of Rome, his concrete way of loving the Church, and his acceptance of the necessity to suffer by and for Her.

On the day of Brother Roger's funeral a banner was seen proclaiming, "Sainthood Now!" The use of this expression directly linked him to Pope John Paul II, whose friend he had been. "Sainthood Now!" As someone who first received the Gospel in a family of Reformed Christians, that would certainly have embarrassed him. It also might have worried him, because he was so anxious not to wound anyone else's conscience, and never wished to *"renounce anything of the faith of his origins in the process of reconciling it with the mystery of the Catholic faith."* The banner bore witness to Brother Roger's place in the Church today and in the hearts of so many men and women in a different, but just as genuine, way as the man whom he loved to refer to as *"the beloved Pope John Paul II."*

Such is the measure of the enormous gratitude for this figure of paternal and kind authority, of openness and faithfulness, of authenticity and courage.

A way of life is open, an invitation to grapple with trust which will guide us through these fifteen days of prayer with Brother Roger.

1
The Humble Sign of a Community

When a common prayer foreshadows heaven's joy here on earth, people come running from everywhere to discover what unconsciously they have been longing for. Nothing is more conducive to a communion with the living God than a meditative common prayer with, as its high point, singing that never ends and that continues in the silence of one's heart when one is alone again. The winds may blow, scorching us in their passage and expanding our inner deserts ... but here our unslaked thirsts will be satisfied. (LF)

*M*erely saying the name Taizé conjures up gatherings and times of prayer in parishes as well as in exhibition halls during large meetings in European cities or on other continents. Are people aware that Taizé is actually the name of a monastic community in Burgundy, France?

To pray: sometimes this word intimidates us. Whether or not we already know Christ, we often find ourselves like the disciples, beseeching: "Lord, teach us to pray!" (Luke 11:1). We are overwhelmed by a great desire to pray, and yet may find ourselves inhibited by our ignorance of how to do so. Without waiting for the Lord to respond, or without knowing how to figure it out for ourselves, we try to put together a fragment here, another fragment there, until a moment comes when we encounter others on the way, who become witnesses for us, guides who help us to focus on Christ and who help us put words to the realities of our inner life. For many people, Brother Roger was and remains one of those witnesses. But not himself alone, not in isolation. How then? By his commitment to praying with others.

In order to allow a road to open for us through him, let us begin by joining him at Taizé, at the place where his youthful intuition crystallized and took shape in 1940 as an unprecedented venture. Descendant of a family of old Protestant stock, unexpectedly he wanted to gather men whom God was calling to live together in order to be *"a leaven of reconciliation in the communion which is the Church"* (DSF).

As a child at home with his family, he had listened to selections from the history of Port-Royal, by Sainte-Beuve. Rather than absorbing the strict scrupulosity of the Jansenism inspiring it, what impressed him was the spiritual adventure which had been lived out at the Abbey of Port-Royal des Champs, not far from Paris, in the 17th century. The personal conversion of a very young woman, Angélique Arnaud, had not only transformed the atmosphere of the monastery, but overflowed to influence the world beyond it. Pascal, Racine, and many other notables became regular attendants at the abbey. A group of them, called The Solitaries, without ever taking vows, nonetheless came to this center of gospel life for inner renewal. He wrote:

> *Personally, I was captivated to discover what a few women, living in community, had been able to accomplish. Close to our house there was a large yew tree with very dense foliage. One day when I was about sixteen I stopped by that tree and said to myself: "If those few women, responding with great clarity to a call to community life and giving their life for Christ, had so much impact on those around them, could not a few men, living in community, do the same thing?"* (GLA)

Without yet knowing its exact shape, he carried this call within him more strongly than ever when he set out at age 25. His theological studies gave him an opportunity to test his intuition and to investigate the gospel foundations of monastic life. The title of his thesis was, "The monastic ideal up until St. Benedict and its reflection of the Gospel."

A Mystical Geography

Spurred by a sense of urgency, even in the midst of a war, he left Switzerland and came to France; here he entered a country humiliated by defeat, poor and chaotic. He had resolutely armed himself only with the weapons of the Gospel. Without disassociating himself from worldly battles, he chose to rely above all else on the power of prayer. On his way, he came upon Taizé, a small village in Burgundy, a place Brother Roger ultimately chose because he knew that God was waiting there for him.

Taizé was isolated, deserted, a suitable place of retreat. Life there was hard; the house he had found was in deplorable condition. But the location evoked a mystical geography. Very close to Cluny, one would be living near the ancient Benedictine abbey whose influence had radiated throughout all of Europe; close also to Cîteaux, the motherhouse of the Abbey of Port-Royal.... At Taizé he decisively accepted the insistent invitation of an old woman to share her meal with him. Having gone out, like Abraham, without knowing where he would set down roots for his project, he recognized in her welcome a sign being made to him by Christ.

Although he began all alone at Taizé, Brother Roger already used the communal "we" in a booklet printed in 1941, *Explanatory Notes*, which he signed The Community of Cluny. Astonishing prophecy! In 1944 he published an expanded article titled *Introduction to Community Life*. During his university studies he had listened closely to his fellow students and saw clearly their common yearning to break out of a spirituality that was too individualistic. He was struck by how isolated these fervent young Christians felt themselves to be. Solitude may be an essential condition of an inner life, but isolation is not.

He was still all alone, but he knew that his desire to create a *"parable of community"* (ST) was shared by others. Finally, however, the upheavals of history meant that the longed-for community life and prayer would begin in Geneva. Taizé was not far from the line of demarcation dividing the occupied zone from Vichy, France, and Brother Roger had been sheltering refugees, Jews among them. He was denounced to the Gestapo and had to retreat to Geneva. But this was hardly wasted time! His plans for community life began to take shape there and aroused the enthusiasm of the first brothers.

Today Taizé has become a symbolic place which sounds to us like a family name: it resonates within us, "Brother Roger of Taizé…." And that name itself echoes worldwide! Three times a day the bells ring out, inviting us to prayer, a prayer unfolding in every language within a simple, spare liturgy. Common prayer, the faithful presence of the community, is the rock upon which the Lord establishes our own personal prayer. In the Church of the

Reconciliation, the long file of almost a hundred brothers unfurls within the central space, and by its presence supports the surrounding crowd. Brother Roger himself is no longer there to greet them, but "the legacy lives!" In the words of his successor, Brother Alois, *"the humble sign of a community"* (DP) still lives and continues to invite us.

Wherever we are, we can ask ourselves what possibilities exist in our lives for a community to support our own prayer life. To respond to Christ's invitation, and perhaps with only two or three others to establish a community and break out of our isolation, without being discouraged by small beginnings. *"A sung prayer with others allows the desire for God to well up in us and helps us enter into contemplative waiting"* (GH).

"De noche iremos, de noche que para encontrar la fuente, solo la sed nos alumbra."

"By night we hasten, in darkness, to search for living water. Only our thirst leads us onward."

Music: Jacques Berthier (1923–1994)
© Ateliers et Presses de Taizé

Reflection Questions

What helps me to realize that faith in Christ is a communal and not an individualistic reality? Who are the people who have helped me find a deeper relationship with God? Do I find support in my local parish or congregation? In what way can I be present for others as a witness to faith?

2

Kindle the Flame That Never Dies Away

For as long as we can go back in history, vast numbers of believers have known that, in prayer, God brings a light, a life within.

Long before Christ, one believer prayed: "My soul longs for you by night, Lord; deep within me, my spirit seeks you."

A desire for a communion with God has lain within the human heart from endless ages of time. The mystery of that communion touches the most inward, the very inmost depths of our being.

So we can say to Christ: "To whom else should we go, other than you? You have the words that bring our souls to life." (PSH)

*I*n the course of his writings Brother Roger revealed the fruits of his spiritual experience. Little by little we discover recurring allusions to his own life of prayer, to the important stages of his life, to this event or to those words of Scripture. His vocation as prior of the Taizé Community kept him in touch not only with the spiritual development of his brothers, but also with a great variety of men and women who confided in him. From such experience he shaped a mystical vision of the human person: whether we are aware of it or not, in us and for us Christ is quietly praying. The prayer which arises within us does not come from us. We do not give it form by some technique which we can acquire by training. To try is to run "*a risk of encountering a God manufactured out of our own human projections*" (HT).

At the beginning of every journey into the inner life lies, not a method, but an intuition to be confirmed, an act of faith: but in all this, it is God who takes the first step. "I believe; help my unbelief!" (Mark 9:24). The Creator remains attached to the man or woman whom he has made in his own image, and in whom he recognizes the image of his Son. Always going before us is the gift of his "Spirit who intercedes with sighs too deep for words" (Romans 8:26). God loves us first, and places deep within us this longing for eternity which sets us in motion, this yearning of one heart for another which allowed Moses to converse with God "as one speaks to a friend" (Exodus 33:11).

But what do we do when this yearning finds no perceptible resonance in us? When we are insecure in our faith, or when it seems so fragile? Brother Roger knew such dark days as well. He remembered very clearly his youthful difficulties, when he went through a time of severe doubt. It was not God's existence that he called into question, but rather his own capacity to experience the presence of an apparently silent God. In his childhood he had tasted the beauty of the world of faith. The confusions and humiliations of adolescence had led later to a loss of faith. He read the Bible regularly; he studied theology. And still many questions arose within him.

A time came when prayer seemed totally beyond him, unattainable. This continued until the day when, overwhelmed by the possibility of losing his dearly loved sister Lily, these words of the Psalmist welled up in his heart: "Come, my heart says, seek his face! Your face, Lord, do I seek" (Psalm 27). From this foundational experience, Brother Roger always retained a sense of kinship with those who feel themselves cut off from any possibility of praying, imprisoned by feelings of unworthiness which get in the way of their inner life. It is not so much that God is silent, as that we hide ourselves behind a veil.

He Is in Our Midst,
But We Do Not Know Him

The question then becomes: how can we reconnect with God's prayer within us? Jacob slept at Bethel (Genesis 28:11–16). There, in the solitude of sleep, the ladder appeared which joined within him earth and his God. This fugitive discovered that he was the true heir of the covenant made with his father. Elijah was lifted out of his depression and fed by an angel who told him to go out into the desert. There he was expecting a spectacular manifestation of God at Horeb (1 Kings 19:3–18). But he was forced to recognize his mistake, and was surprised by the God who actually spoke to him. *"He understood that the voice of God speaks also in a whisper of silence"* (PH). Our God never wishes to impose himself.

We need only place ourselves in front of God, in his presence. To remain there without being afraid to face the silence. Silence around us, silence within us. *"God of all eternity, we long to seek for you amidst the silences of prayer and live by the hope discovered in the Gospel"* (PSH).

At Taizé we find times and spaces especially set aside for such silence, but more importantly silence dwells at the very heart of the liturgy itself, a silence nourished by the Word of God which has just been read. Not a break in the rhythm of the Office, but rather its fulfillment. The silence is its true heart. It is a kind of musical silence, like a rest, which allows

for dialogue because it awaits a presence, the
silence of an encounter or of the desire for an
encounter and not the silence of emptiness. A
great company in silence together, the community offering itself up to the Word which
can make our lives fruitful. A silence which
lifts us out of time, even when nothing seems
to be happening.

This same silence, when experienced all
alone, involves the risk of listening simply to our
own voice, or of allowing ourselves to become
discouraged or even drowned by feeling unable
to pray. That is the moment to sing these words
of St. Augustine:

*"Jésus le Christ, lumière intérieure, ne laisse pas
mes ténèbres me parler. Jésus le Christ, lumière
intérieure, donne-moi d'accueillir ton amour."*

*"Lord Jesus Christ, your light shines within us,
let not my doubts or my darkness speak to me.
Lord Jesus Christ, your light shines within us; let
my heart always welcome your love."*

Musique: Jacques Berthier (1923–1994),
©Ateliers et Presses de Taizé

Neither our doubts nor our impressions of God's silence can take the Holy Spirit away from us.

Again and again Brother Roger reminds us of the many forms prayer can take: a multitude of words, as in the prayer of Teresa of Avila, because one can say everything to God; invocations repeated over and over in the manner of the Russian pilgrim; short snatches of chants which allow the gospel to penetrate our awareness.... Quoting Saint Augustine, he invites us not to worry about the value of our poor prayer at those times when we feel only silence and "our lips are closed." *"Then we are silent and our heart speaks"* (GH). And then we remain, simply trusting humbly in the elusive language of the heart to fill in the gaps.

There may be gestures that we can find to speak for us.

> *At certain periods I sense that I pray more with my body than my understanding. Such prayer is at ground level — on one's knees, or bowing low, looking at the place where the Eucharist is celebrated, taking advantage of the peaceful silence and even of the sounds coming up from the village. The body is well and truly present to listen, grasp, love.* (F)

Step by step, we discover a personal prayer of our whole being which also incorporates a great diversity of traditional postures.

God of every human being, when we simply
desire to welcome your love, a flame rises up
little by little deep in our souls. Very fragile
though it be, it always keeps burning. (PSH)

Reflection Questions

Am I afraid of silence? Have I ever realized
that prayer is not something that I *do*, but rather
God's presence at work within me? What does
it mean to believe in a God who never imposes
himself? What ways can I find to pray with the
body as well as the mind?

3
Returning to the Spirit of Childhood

To allow Christ to penetrate into our most impenetrable depths is to return endlessly to the spirit of childhood. This does not prevent us from becoming adults; in no way does it lead to childishness.

To be ourselves, without disguises, without tricks: nothing so distorts communion, or destroys the integrity of a person, as wearing masks. (VP)

*T*o probe what lies deep in the human heart, in its most secret recesses…. There is something fascinating about its complexity, as there is about its mysterious genesis. Mindful of his own personal history and that of those around him in order to seek God's footprints there, Brother Roger had a long-standing interest in the psychology of the innermost depths. Several times in his journal he mentions conversations with a psychiatrist friend whose wisdom and humility he admired. But he was wary of *"analytical notions only half-understood"* and those who play at being *"the great experts and wreak their havoc"* (LND), even to encouraging harsh feelings against a father or a mother, and to keeping alive bitterness or jealousies.

A spirit of faith, without denying psychic suffering, can allow a different approach toward it, without being swept away by disastrous soul-searching.

> *When introspection and analysis turn a man in on himself, what destruction that brings! Who then will open for him the gateways of praise? ... The gateways of praise give passage to deathly anguish and to songs unending. God will set his mark on the very wounds themselves, making them no longer torment, but energy for communion.* (LND)

Suppose That the Ultimate Meaning of Life Were the Joy of God in Us All?

All that is necessary to be healed and freed from ourselves is to return to the spirit of child-hood: spontaneity and inner freedom....

> *God of all tenderness, you come and make of us the humble ones of the Gospel. We are so eager to understand that the best of us is built up by means of a very simple trust that even a child can achieve.* (PSH)

Paradoxically, far from being "natural," this approach is the fruit of a victory. One senses that it took a long period of maturation to free Brother Roger from what might have become a severe and austere spirit, and to liberate him from worrying about what other people might say.

Latent Puritanism is always hoping to kill life. It blushes at spontaneity. It wishes to murder the soul, and disguises as positive necessity that which is nothing but destructive anger. (WL)

In 1968, when he was already over 50 years old, he published selections from his journal in which he wrote candidly:

When the time comes to address a crowd of people, in order to overcome my shyness I say to myself: Stand there like a child, the child you once were when your oldest sister taught you to read and write. (DSF)

To become a person of blessings.... The truth of the Gospel is on the side of generosity of life, and a naked vulnerability transformed into strength, vulnerability "that he cultivated like a door through which God can choose to come in and be close to us," in words written by the Prior of the Grande Chartreuse at Brother Roger's death. *"Praise to the Risen Christ who, knowing how poor and vulnerable we are, comes and prays in us the hymn of his unchanging confidence"* (DSF).

Didn't Christ make plain his preference for children (Matthew 18:3)? Doesn't the Kingdom belong to children, and those who are like them (Matthew 19:13–14)? Anxious to avoid the risk of over-intellectualizing sometimes encountered in the Church, and striving to recapture his childhood intuitions, Brother Roger was quick to hold serious conversations with children he met. For their sake he regularly visited toy stores, and kept a supply of candies on hand to share with them. Sometimes their reactions surprised him, and he enjoyed trying to figure out their often prosaic meanings. He loved to laugh. With infinite respect and great compassion, he also echoed their sorrows without minimizing them.

> *Be thankful for the reflection of your face in the child who reveals for us your mysterious presence, which opens us to the realities of the Kingdom, an overflowing heart, simplicity, wonder, jubilation.* (DSF)

These words echo Christ's astonishment when he was moved to exclaim: "I thank you, Father, because you have hidden these things from the wise and the intelligent and have revealed them to infants" (Luke 10:21).

To maintain such an inner attitude, and as a reminder of what all of us are asked to try and live, during the prayer children clustered in a jumble around Brother Roger and, candles in hand, helped to pass on the Easter light during the prayer each Saturday evening. Children: the nearness of the Kingdom, the promise that God is bringing something new to birth in our lives.

Walking Toward Astonishment, Toward the Unhoped-for

To pull off our masks, or not to take them seriously, doesn't mean being naive or mal-adjusted to social life. We know that, con-sciously or not, we are often part of the social game, even within the Church. We can try not to be a part of this game while still remaining in touch with practical reality and a sense of our responsibilities.

> *The spirit of childhood is a crystal-clear way of looking and, far from being simplistic, it is lucid as well. The various aspects of a situa-tion, positive and negative, are no strangers to it. It has nothing childish about it. It is imbued with maturity. It requires infinite courage.*
> *The spirit of childhood does not let itself be held back by the hardened structures of the Church. It looks for ways of getting through them, as a stream of water finds its way through the frozen earth in early spring.* (LF)

The adult Nicodemus asked Jesus how to be born again (cf. John 3:4).... And, poking fun at theological knowledge disconnected from a lived life of theological virtues, Christ offers us faith in the elusive action of the Holy Spirit who makes all things new. Looking through the eyes of a child makes it possible to discover a whole world within each new day, to receive it as a gift, to contemplate it with love.

Creation becomes the herald of the Living God. How can a person not pay attention to it? And how then can he not be moved to praise it? And when that person is Brother Roger, how not be inspired to poetry?

> *Enchanting, all that the eyes take in. The coolness of the brief showers. Sunshine again, and each blade of grass has come alive. The happiness of the springtimes of childhood. Setbacks and shadows are washed by the fine rain, swept away by the hot light of a copper sunbeam. And the race begins all over again, leaps for joy alternating with expectations disappointed. In these little things a zest for life is engraved like filigree, a source without which everything would be insipid.* (WL)

"Seigneur, tu gardes mon âme. Ö Dieu, to connais mon cœur. Conduis-moi sur le chemin d'éternité. Conduis-moi sur le chemin d'éternité."

Seigneur, tu gardes mon âme

"O Lord, you hold and protect me; you know all my heart's desire. Guide my steps along the everlasting way."

Music: Taizé, © Ateliers et Presses de Taizé

Reflection Questions

How would I define the spirit of childhood? Is it possible to reconcile a childlike spirit with a mature attitude towards life? What kind of masks do I wear? Does prayer help me to remove them?

4
God Is Love Alone

In the presence of physical violence or moral torture in the human family, a question plagues us: if God is love, where does evil come from?

God does not stand by passively at the pain of human beings; he suffers with the innocent, victims of incomprehensible ordeals; he suffers with everyone. There is a pain God suffers, a pain Christ suffers. In the Gospel, Christ enters into solidarity with the suffering; he weeps at the death of someone he loves.

Did not Christ come to earth so that every human being might know that he or she is loved?

And our hearts can awaken to the wonder of a love. (GLA)

*O*ne witness is perhaps enough to touch us in our very depths. Before it became a call to community life, the story of Angélique Arnauld, the Abbess of Port-Royal, which he had already heard when still a child, enabled the young Roger to understand that *"God loves us* *before we love him"* (GLA). A decisive experience, which he reclaimed as an adult, and worked tirelessly to share so that everyone might be placed in their proper vocation of praise.

He who invites us so strongly to connect with our childhood hearts rarely invoked God as father-figure. Did the memory of his own father's authoritarianism, which he found so distressing, mark him for life? In the prayers which he wrote to be read during the common prayer in the church, he rarely invoked the Father, but rather God, Jesus the Christ, or the Holy Spirit. The filial trust which he displayed had been transmitted to him by his mother.

There are mothers who, in the life of their child, leave an indelible imprint and remain an unwavering support. (GLA)

Until his final days, Brother Roger sought tirelessly to lead us back to that fundamental reality: the goodness of God. Do we truly believe that God loves each one of us *"with an eternal love"*? He was always deeply affected when frightening ideas were expressed in his presence which could act upon certain sensibilities and confuse their spiritual lives: ideas like an arbitrary all-powerful God who imposes his will; the prospect of a judgment based on moral perfection; a call to sanctity heard as a "mission impossible" and, given human frailty, presupposing inevitable condemnation.

God Never Forces Himself on Us, Creating Fear

Such a caricature of God perpetuates itself in certain circles, including Christian ones, and the problem of evil is thereby aggravated for non-believers: how can one rely on a distant God who allows people to face so many misfortunes and unmerited sufferings? On the contrary, Brother Roger insisted:

> *What draws us to God is his humble presence. He never wounds human dignity. Any authoritarian act disfigures his face. The impression that God comes to punish is one of the greatest obstacles to faith.* (ST)

To respond to this indictment of God so widespread in our world and so frequently uttered in private, Brother Roger shared his meditations on the Scriptures. He recalled the plight of Job, coming back to this intuition often repeated in a chant of the Taizé Community: "I know that my Redeemer lives, and that at the last he will stand upon the earth; and in my flesh I shall see God, whom I shall see on my side. My heart faints within me!" (Job 19:25). As if echoing that thought, he often told about an experience which had profoundly moved him in a leprosarium in Calcutta: a severely afflicted leper raised what remained of his arms and began to sing. *"God has not inflicted a punishment on me; I praise him because my illness has turned into a visit from God"* (WL).

How marvelous is this faith and this recognition of a God who accompanies human beings, who joins us in our trials. Brother Roger loved to repeat that *"in Jesus, 'God is united to every human being without exception,'"* restating in his own manner the words of the Second Vatican Council in *Gaudium et Spes.*

In My Ordeals, God Is Looking for Me

In the Church of the Reconciliation there is an icon of Coptic origin which says the same thing in its own fashion. It evokes the unfailing companionship which Christ offers to each one of us in times of consolation as well as in times of distress. In it, Christ is shown accompanying the Abbot Mena. As he entrusts a mission of blessing to him, he puts his arm around the abbot's shoulders, thereby transmitting all the force of his brotherly friendship. To contemplate in this way Christ's connection with every person reveals to us something about the heart of God.

> *God came himself upon the earth as a poor man, as a humble man. He came through Christ Jesus. God would indeed be very distant if he were not made visible through Christ.*
> *From the beginning Christ was in God. Since the birth of humanity, he was the Living Word. He came upon the earth to*

make accessible the trusting of faith. Risen
from the dead, he makes his home within us;
he dwells in us through the Holy Spirit. And
we discover that the love of Christ expresses
itself above all by his forgiveness and by his
continuing presence within us. (SHG)

Jesus was a good friend of Lazarus and his family (John 12). But, when he was informed of his illness, he did not prevent Lazarus from dying. He endured the reproaches of the sisters who were also his friends, Martha and Mary. They clearly felt that the friendship had been betrayed: "If you had been here ..." Yet against the advice of his disciples, and moved by the death of his friend, he risked coming to share their mourning, and he wept with them. He did this out of friendship. To travel to Jerusalem was to walk toward his Passion. Such was the mission which the Father had entrusted to him: to share fully in our human condition, to allow himself to be touched by every suffering that touches us.

Christ never stands by passively while some-
one suffers. Risen from the dead, he accom-
panies each of us in our suffering to the
point that God sorrows, that Christ sorrows.
And, in his name, he enables us to share the
distress of those who are undergoing incom-
prehensible trials; he leads us to alleviate the
misery of the innocent. (SHG)

Let us keep our eyes fixed upon Christ who himself knew the feeling of abandonment, who tasted the loneliness of suffering. In the agony at Gethsemane he experienced human abandonment as well as God's silence. He joins us in the today of his resurrection: he is here among us, accompanying us, urgently inviting us to believe in his love which is for all time.

Lord Christ ... you love us.
By taking everything upon your shoulders,
you open for us a way towards the peace of
God. And God never wills suffering, nor
death, nor human distress. He tells us over
and over again: "My love for you will never
disappear." (DSF)

Dieu ne peut que donner son amour. Notre Dieu est tendresse.

"God can only give faithful love: tenderness and forgiveness!"

Music: Joseph Gelineau, © Ateliers et Presses de Taizé

Reflection Questions

What does it mean to believe in a God who is "love alone"? Have I been affected by images of God, perhaps from my childhood, which distorted his true identity and caused me to fear? In what way can prayer help to purify my vision of God? How does the figure of Jesus in the Gospels help me to discover a God of compassion and tenderness?

5
A Yes for a Lifetime

Holy Spirit, although no one is apparently built to live out a yes forever, you come to kindle within me a source of light. You illuminate my hesitations and doubts at those times when the yes and the no clash.

Holy Spirit, you enable me to consent to my own limits. If there is an element of frailty within me, may your presence come and transfigure it.

And thus we are led to the audacity of a yes that will take us very far.

This yes is limpid trusting.

This yes is the love in all our loving. (L2004)

What then is this call to a yes which so regularly punctuates Brother Roger's messages to young people? It is an urgent matter: to respond to love with love. To allow ourselves to be caught up in the insistent invitation which Christ tirelessly offers all of us, just as he does to the rich young man or to Peter: "If you want ..." (Matthew 19:21), "You, follow me!" (John 21:22). This yes is to be yearned for and gathered as the fruit of trust: is it not Christ himself, by his Spirit, who inspires us and gives us strength? Liberty and consideration are part of God's approach, but so too is insistence.

> *Choosing Christ! He confronts us with an alternative: "Whoever wants to save his life will lose it. Whoever gives his life for love of me will find it." But he does not impose the choice. He leaves each one free to choose him or reject him. He never forces us. Simply, gentle and humble of heart, he has been standing for two thousand years at the door of every human heart and knocking: "Do you love me?"*
> *When it seems that the ability to respond to him has disappeared, we can only call out: "Give me the gift to give myself, to rest in you, O Christ, in body and in spirit."* (DF)

Even in his pamphlet of 1941, when he was still alone at Taizé, one senses that Brother Roger was already thinking about a life-commitment, but the time was not yet ripe for him to dare to affirm it. In a footnote he writes: *"We are often asked this question: Are you going to create a permanent community in this house? It is too burning a question today to be able to give any details on the subject"* (EN). It must be noted that since the Reformation there has existed a real suspicion in Protestantism regarding monastic vows.

But how can a permanent community be envisioned without a long-term commitment?

There can be calls that dazzle like flashes of lightning, but more often the discovery of our vocation comes about by small strokes, little by little. Each journey is unique, passing through recognition and acceptance of oneself as the beloved of God, and bearer of a unique name which is revealed to us in prayer and contemplation.

> *In the Gospel, to be oneself means searching deeply until the irreplaceable gift given to each one of us is revealed. Through that special gift, unlike anyone else's, each person is brought to fulfillment in God. To keep silent, to withdraw to the desert in order to recognize this gift, even if only once in a lifetime.* (LND)

In the Seventies, young people attending large Taizé meetings could buy a simple pendant of baked clay with one stroke of blue glaze at its center: the brothers designed it to evoke the white stone of the Apocalypse, on which is inscribed a new name known only to the one receiving it from God (Apocalypse 2:17). It was a double sign, both of a great longing for a personal relationship with Christ, and of membership in a people striving for the coming of the Kingdom. *"To fulfill yourself? Become what you are in your heart of hearts ... and the gates of childhood open up, the wonder of a love"* (WL).

Resolve and Don't Turn Back

At Taizé, a radical offering of one's life is beyond doubt the beginning of everything. But things had to go forward with prudence. In 1944, in his *Introduction to Community Life,* Brother Roger took pains to quote a substantial passage from Luther who, despite everything, left open the possibility of monasteries as places of formation, especially for liturgy. The founder of Taizé thereby placed himself in a continuum with the Church at the very moment when he was beginning to do something new....

> *Confronted with Eternity's endless loving, we sense that our real response cannot be temporary, just for a while, before we resume the old life once more. Neither can our response be a mere effort of will. This would break certain people. Rather it means surrendering ourselves.* (LND)

In his dissertation of 1943, Brother Roger wrote that a commitment for a lifetime was not possible, but that the truth of love bears within itself the intention of not turning back. Everything led the first brothers to give a definite shape to the commitment they were already living, to say the yes which the Spirit had already planted in their hearts. However, they still needed to conquer their misgivings: will we be capable of maintaining a lifetime commitment? What will happen in those dark times which will inevitably occur? Brother Roger trusted a woman of great faith, a Protestant theologian, and he relates that she said to him:

"You are afraid you won't be able to persevere? But the Holy Spirit is there, strong enough to uphold a vocation for an entire lifetime" (GH).

So it was that at Easter 1949, the first seven brothers made their profession, discovering in it the unique liberty and intimate joy given by a life rooted, not in their own resources, but in the faithfulness of God. They then pledged themselves always to hold all material and spiritual goods in common, to live in the availability made possible by celibacy, and to recognize the authority of the prior as the minister of the community.... *"Yes, the wonder of a joy! The Gospel bears within it such a bright hope that we would like to go even to the point of giving ourselves in order to communicate it"* (GH).

Like Christ's disciples, however small our initial yes may be, over time this yes becomes truly a fullness. God calls us to happiness and growth in humanity, not to frustration or dehumanizing actions.

> *Jesus, our hope, your Gospel enables us to sense that, even in dark times, God wants us to be happy. And the peace in our hearts can make life beautiful for those around us.* (PSH)

Joy! The inner light of a countenance which, until the end of his days, inspired trust and faithfulness. Thus Brother Roger continued to witness in the evening in the church even when he scarcely had strength enough for a real dialogue. To allow this yes to ring out within our very depths is also to follow in the steps of Mary, to the rhythm of the Spirit, and all at once we discover in the "forever" a path of rejoicing which invites us to sing along with her:

"Magnificat, magnificat, magnificat anima mea Dominum!"

"My soul praises the Lord."

Music: Jacques Berthier (1923–1994)
©Ateliers et Presses de Taizé

God our Father, we want to love you with all our strength, with all our soul. But you know that there can be within us inner resistances. Give us the boldness to leap over the walls, to dare to renew again and for always the yes of the gift of our whole life. (PH)

Reflection Questions

Does the idea of a lifetime commitment frighten me? Is it possible in a world where everything is constantly changing? How do I live out the definitive yes of my baptism in the circumstances of my life? What elements have changed in my life of faith over the years, and what elements have remained constant?

6
Happy the Simple-Hearted!

One of the first things Christ says in the Gospel is this: "Happy the simple-hearted!" Yes, happy those who head towards simplicity, simplicity of heart and simplicity of life. A simple heart strives to live in the present moment, to welcome each day as God's today. Does not the spirit of simplicity shine out in serene joy, and even in cheerfulness? Simplifying our life enables us to share with the least fortunate, in order to alleviate suffering where there is disease, poverty, famine. (GH)

*B*rother Roger estimated that he was 18 years old when he began to search for those few words of Scripture which he wanted to make his own priorities, and he invites us to do the same. He began to set them down first for himself, then for his brothers, and finally, more widely still, for all those for whom such an approach can be helpful: for young people visiting the hill of Taizé, for readers of his writings. Unceasingly he meditated on them. He made them his own, wrote them in his own style and then rewrote them, always striving for the simplest expressions, those which can easily be recalled, to strike the mind and touch the heart and dwell within us once and for all.

> *A person can only shape him- or herself, the unity of the personality can only be built upon a few basic reference-points to which one constantly returns. These guidelines, which were worked out gradually, formed our original "rule," our first sources.* (DSF)

The essential elements held in common by the Community, at its heart of hearts, can be found clearly stated in these three principles formulated in 1941, the third of which was taken from the Protestant Third Order of Sentinels:

> *Throughout your day, let work and rest be quickened by the Word of God. Keep inner silence in all things so as to dwell in Christ. Be filled with the spirit of the Beatitudes: joy, simplicity, mercy.* (EN)

They can be found again in the Rule of Taizé, the formulation of which was nourished by the experiences of the Community's early days. The Rule is nothing like a constitution or a legal text, but is actually a small treatise on the spiritual life. Since 1953 its form has become simpler still, to the point of being called *"the little source"* (ST).

A Gospel Way

"Each one of us carries within himself a great inner theme. Let it sing and go on singing. It is useless to look elsewhere. A continuous creation is born of that" (DSF). Ever since his thesis on monastic life and its conformity with the Gospel, Brother Roger had always had the same concern: to look for Gospel values where they are being lived out and to search everywhere for the *"source,"* that image that spoke so powerfully to him, with great freedom of spirit and generosity of heart, without being taken in by appearances, and without any preconceived notions. What matters is to seek Christ where he actually is.

To seek him out even in Rome, should the occasion arise! This happened in 1949, thanks to Cardinal Gerlier, who facilitated meetings with Pope Pius XII and the future Pope Paul VI.

It was perhaps a similar simplicity in the two men which fostered Brother Roger's special relationship with Pope John XXIII, who once exclaimed: *"Ah, Taizé, that little springtime!"* Once Brother Roger asked Pope John why he trusted him so much, to which the Pope responded, "You have innocent eyes" (CL). And in an expression of mutual trust, the Prior of Taizé wrote about John XXIII: *"He was himself so transparent that one could read him like an open book"* (KS).

In its radicalism, the figure of Saint Francis of Assisi fascinated Brother Roger: poverty, joy, poetry, a keen sense of the suffering of the Church and commitment to her. But, to preserve its freedom, the Community of Taizé was never a mendicant order. "From the start we felt obliged never to accept gifts, either in money or in kind" (DSF). He often recalled his last meeting with his father who, as a pastor, had seen what went on in parishes and worried about the Community possibly becoming dependent upon donors. *"I remember giving him then the same answer: 'From the first day, when I was alone at Taizé, I lived from the work of my own hands and, with this in mind, I learned among other things, to milk cows'"* (DSF).

The little bit of land the Community owned permitted agricultural activities, which the first brothers undertook, not without risks. But always the question was: *"Who are, right now, the disadvantaged around us?"* (CL). In 1961 the encyclical *Mater et Magistra,* which urged small farmers to join together and organize, found a special resonance in the Taizé brothers. The Community entered into this movement and, with several farmers of the region, participated in a cooperative, the Copex.

> *Each day's distribution made real the petition for our daily bread; it allowed us to enter into the meaning of the provisional in the childlike spirit of the Beatitudes.* (DP)

Arranging Everything in the Simple Beauty of Creation

A woman in the Hebrew Scriptures pointed the way, a widow of Zarephath (1 Kings 17:7–16). In a time of drought and famine, with a son to feed, her supply of food was nearly exhausted. Nevertheless she answered the request for food of Elijah, the man whom God had sent to her, and shared her bare minimum with him. *"She pushes her trust to the utmost limits, at which point, in a flash, God intervenes. The flour and the oil will never give out"* (LND).

When we allow ourselves to be shaped in the form of Jesus Christ, born poor among the poor, glorification of poverty can become a temptation. Brother Roger often preferred to substitute the word "simplicity" for "poverty," so much did he mistrust anything which might induce puritanical guilt-feelings when the true concern is *"choosing God as our first love"* (DSF).

On the contrary, he invites us always to keep a sense of beauty and of celebration, to look for whatever can cheer us, to nourish praise, to maintain our love of life.... *"Simplicity devoid of burning charity is a shadow without light"* (ST).

Paradoxically, this same simplicity led him to accept certain prizes and awards. He saw in them a recognition and encouragement for the way of reconciliation which he was traveling with his community. Wasn't this also an opportunity of witnessing in different social circles? The money received was immediately distributed to people in need.

In simplicity, without looking back, let us welcome the gifts of God and share them.

> *Next to you, Jesus Christ, it becomes possible to know God, in allowing the little we understand of the Gospel to enter into our own lives. And that little is just enough to keep us going forward day after day. You never turn us into a people who "have made it." We live our whole lives as Christ's poor people who, in all simplicity, dispose ourselves to trust in the mystery of faith.* (SHG)

"Nada te turbe, nada te espante, quien a Dios tiene, nada le falta. Nada te turbe, nada te espante, solo Dios basta."

Nada te turbe

"Nothing can trouble, nothing can frighten. Those who seek God shall never go wanting. God alone fills us" (Teresa of Avila).

Music: Jacques Berthier (1923–1994),
© Ateliers et Presses de Taizé

Reflection Questions

Are there a few inner priorities which have always marked my life? Can I formulate them? Do I hear the call to live more simply? How can my life become less cluttered, more focused on what really matters? What can I let go of? How can a simple life remain joyful and not austere?

7
Living God's Today

People who strive to surrender themselves to God body and soul let themselves be built up from within on the basis of a few simple truths from the Gospel.... For those who wait patiently, during their own necessary maturing the day comes when their inner selves have been refashioned without their even realizing it.

Those who surrender themselves to the Spirit of the living God do not focus their attention on their advances or their setbacks. They go forward as if walking along a narrow ridge, forgetting what lies behind. They do not try to measure imperceptible inner changes. They do not know how, but day and night the seed sprouts and grows....

To keep up our spirits, let us welcome at each dawn the coming day. In each of us God is doing a new thing.

Living God's today, that is the most important thing. Tomorrow will be another today.
(LF)

To fulfill and not to do away with.... From the beginning Brother Roger had certain key intuitions which shaped the adventure of Taizé's communal life and its impact on the Church. But as the bearer of a project whose import went far beyond himself, he had no detailed outline for accomplishing it, because such an outline could not come from him. God does not turn us into strategists, not even as apostles. He had to go forward by trial and error, often faced with great misunderstanding from both the Catholic and the Reformed churches.

He wanted to reconnect with *"the first flowering of the Church"* and the vitality preceding all of its separations. But he knew very well that one can neither fixate on an idealized past nor cling to the description of the first Christian community in the Acts of the Apostles. It is impossible to ignore the contentious legacy of history, nor to avoid coming to grips with the challenges of modern life in order truly to walk alongside people of today.

There were many gratifying encounters along the way, but he still had to confront and come to terms with the full weight and harshness of the reality of "today" which lies between past and future: mistrust, fear, criticism, inertia....

What enabled him to keep going? A disposition toward the future that might be called hope, the conviction in the depths of his heart that Christ had transmitted a mission to his Church, that God does not stop caring about every human being, and does not withdraw from history. At any moment God might burst into our lives and the life of the Church if we take for our own the words of the Psalmist: "Oh, that today you would listen to his voice! Do not harden your hearts" (Psalm 95). And then we enter into God's today.

Your Miracle in Us

Living God's Today: the first book published by the Presses de Taizé was boldly titled, even at the risk of its theme being confused with the instant gratification of contemporary life. *"Christian, you bear the name of Christ; for you every moment can become fullness of life"* (DSF). Far from advocating an individualistic and self-centered approach of "live your own life," the founder of Taizé echoed the call to conversion which runs throughout all of Scripture. Like Zacchaeus, we need only welcome and agree to Christ's coming to us to find ourselves shaken up and transformed, forgiven and restored to the dignity of a Son or Daughter of the Promise, even to the extent of making radical decisions (Luke 19:1–10).

> *Sometimes you ask me where is the source, where is the joy of hoping. I will answer you. All your past, even the moment that has just gone by, is already swallowed up, drowned with Christ in the water of your baptism.*

Don't look back: that is part of a Christian's freedom. He is only interested in running to meet what is to come. Refuse to look back. Not in order to be irresponsible. If you have wounded your neighbor, would you leave him lying on the roadside? Would you refuse reconciliation, refuse to pour oil on his wounds? Refuse to look back. Not in order to forget the best of your past. It is up to you to celebrate the times when God passed through your life, to remember your inner liberations. (DSF)

Left to the demands of his own heart Zacchaeus would have despaired, but lifted up by Christ's gaze he became a different man. Brother Roger understood this well. Memory can make us a slave to keeping count of wounds we have received or mistakes we have made, to brooding over them. It is possible for such imaginings, in an anxious temperament, to subvert the inner life. Wisdom would lead us to cut this process short, to embrace reality without yielding to the imaginary. At such times it is helpful to open our hearts to another person. Such confession exposes us to the light of Christ and allows us to lay down our burdens.

When he forgives us again and again, God is inviting us to blow away remorse itself like a child blowing an autumn leaf. We can be sure of one thing: where there is forgiveness, God is there, always. (DSF)

Cleansing our memories opens a door through which the Spirit can act in us today, transform us and give us life by a forgiveness which we cannot practice all by ourselves. Brother Roger loved to call to mind Saint John of the Cross and Saint Teresa of Avila: they show us that there is no age-limit on beginning a new life. It is never too late to offer ourselves to the transfiguring light of Christ.

Witness to a Different Future

This is the demand of faith if we want to say with Christ: "Forgive us as we forgive..."

> *The word love is so often abused. Living out a love that forgives is another matter.... Forgiving: there lies the secret stimulus that makes you too a witness to a different future.* (DSF)

So also, in the Church, institutional obstacles cannot be allowed the last word. In order to "live God's today," Brother Roger fostered ecumenical meetings, tirelessly seeking to go forward. Pope John XXIII's invitation for observers to the Second Vatican Council sparked a great hope: *"We will not try to find out who was wrong, we will not try to find out who was right, we will only say: let us be reconciled!"* (KS). The two men shared the same intuition.

Responding to the Gospel call to pray for our enemies allows us to enter upon a dynamic of transformation.

No prayer goes unanswered. When we entrust to God those who have hurt us, it may well be that something changes for them, but in any case our own hearts are on the way to peace. (SHG)

To receive mercy, isn't this the blessing promised to the merciful? Forgiving, or asking for forgiveness, creates a new relationship and allows a glimpse of reconciliation. Suddenly we are free, yearning from now on to *"live in the present moment with God"* (DSF).

Holy Spirit, you do not wish us to be anxious; you clothe us in your peace. It prepares us to live each day as a day that belongs to God. (PSH)

"Notre âme attend le Seigneur. En lui la joie de notre cœur."

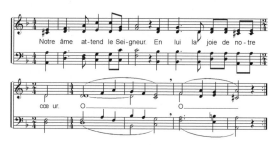

"Our soul is waiting for God. Our hearts find joy in the Lord."

Music: Jacques Berthier (1923–1994),
© Ateliers et Presses de Taizé

Reflection Questions

What keeps me from living in "God's today"? What are the priorities for me here and now? How can the assurance of God's constant forgiveness help me to deal with unfinished business from the past? Do my hopes for the future keep me from living fully in the present moment? Does my prayer life enable me to discover God at work in my life now?

8
A Path Opens

Are you surrounded by things you cannot understand?

When darkness grows deep, his love is a fire. You need only fix your gaze steadily on that lamp burning in the darkness, till day begins to dawn and the sun rises in your heart.

You know very well that you are not the one who creates this source of light; it comes from Christ.

Dazzling visit of the love of God, the Holy Spirit flashes through each human life like lightning in the night. By this mysterious presence, the Risen Christ takes hold of you. He takes everything upon himself, even the trials so hard to bear.

Only later, sometimes much later, will you understand that his overflowing life is never lacking. And you will say: "Was not my heart burning within me while he spoke to me?" (ST)

A friend of Taizé from the beginning, Father Villain, suggested to the brothers the idea of a prayer vestment. Because of shortages at war's end, old sheets were hastily stitched together. But it was Mother Teresa who practically forced Brother Roger to wear his robe almost all the time, as a sign needed by the people of today. Its whiteness recalls the baptismal vocation, when we are clothed in Christ, or the garments worn by the guests at the Wedding of the Lamb of the Apocalypse. It serves to place us always in the light of Easter.

It was, after all, on Easter Day in 1949 when Brother Roger and his first brothers made their life commitment. It was again at Easter in 1970 that the Council of Youth was announced, which later became the Pilgrimage of Trust across the earth. The year in Taizé is calculated from one Easter to the next.

> *Our life of eternity with God does not begin at the moment when we last close our eyes upon this earth....*
>
> *How happy you are! In you the Resurrection has already begun (Colossians 2:10–12). You are already part of a fullness, an eternal love!... Casting off what weighs you down, fix your eyes upon Jesus Christ. He is the source of faith. Let inner light dawn within you like the Morning Star, the Spirit of the Risen Lord. It will shed light on your*

pathway of peaceful trust and, moment by moment, you will understand how to go forward. (Easter 1983)

From Doubt to Hope in God

A man of great sensitivity and committed to harmony, fearful of wounding others and disliking conflict, Brother Roger suffered a great deal, sometimes to barely endurable extremes, as he sometimes implied. It might have been because of difficulties or withdrawals of some of the brothers at the heart of the community or from a sense of his own limitations. In the same way, in the larger community which is the Church, there was resistance and opposition, silence and scorn. While he sought only one thing, to help bring about reconciliation, he saw his intentions distorted, and misunderstandings and obstacles arise instead.

Fully one with the spiritual theology of the Church Fathers, he questioned why some theological discussions focused more on the meanderings of history and past debates than on the search for a common future. Inspired by a vision of the Church and convinced of the urgency of bearing witness, he wanted to show all the aspects of communion which could already be lived out and he was instead accused of not thinking things through. A personal humiliation, yes; but more seriously, it called into question the very meaning of his entire life of service to Church unity. Without regarding himself as a persecuted prophet, he nonetheless knew that in following Christ a disciple was not spared suffering.

Sometimes we may feel that we have reached a dead end, that we have used up all our resources of human hope. Then the words of the Psalmist may rise to our lips: "Why have you forgotten me?... My adversaries taunt me, while they say to me continually, 'Where is your God?'" (Psalm 42). In interpreting this psalm, Brother Roger added: *"In us a gulf of worries calls up another gulf, the boundless compassion of his love. And we are astonished: trust was at hand, and so often we did not realize it"* (PH). It is the Easter experience of death and resurrection being offered to us.

The Living Christ Goes before Us

This was what the disciples had already discovered on the road to Emmaus (Luke 24:13–35). They were good men, swallowed up in their disappointment, and the doubt it cast upon the word of God. Their hope was gone. Then suddenly the Risen Christ met them as they were going home on the evening of Easter. They had believed in Jesus, they remembered the many signs he had performed for them. They had believed that he was the fulfillment of the Promise, but they had come up against the necessity of suffering and had turned away from the Cross. They didn't understand that Love is measured by the Cross, and it is there that the heart of God can be recognized.

They had not yet made the transition. It was night, and their Easter was not achieved until the breaking of the bread, which restored their memory of the message. Good news! It may be late, but there is still time to open our door and invite the stranger to our table, and to welcome the Spirit of the Risen Christ who interprets the Scriptures for us. Brother Roger always came back to this:

> *Whether we know it or not, Christ is along-side every one of us.... And is not our first task to be, for every person, a pointer to the presence of Christ?*
> *He is present in secret, light in our darkness, a burning in the heart.* (Easter 1972)

Easter's light does not diminish the drama lived by so many men, women, and children, which we can only respond to, with Christ, in prayer, without either sentimentality or exalta-tion of suffering. We can live every weekend like a recurring Easter. At Taizé a symbolic gesture brought back from Moscow is enacted every Friday, which is to

> *lay the icon of the cross on the floor, go and place your forehead on the wood of the cross,*

entrust to God, by a prayer of the body, one's own burdens and those of others. In this way keep company with the Risen Christ who continues to be in agony for those in tribulation throughout the world. (DSF)

On Saturday evening, from the single candle which represents Christ, the light is passed from neighbor to neighbor to all the candles just before the reading of the Gospel of the Resurrection. This liturgy is a reminder of the Easter Vigil and, inviting us to a new birth, recalls the meaning of Sunday, the first day of the week, the first day of the new creation.

What does it mean to be born again? It means allowing ourselves to enter along with the Risen Christ into a dynamic of successive transitions.... To allow the Risen Christ to descend into the depths of the human condition to take up our burdens and at a single stroke to arouse us from passivity.... While all our worrying cannot lessen the weight of our burdens, the life offered by the Risen Christ wipes away everything, and draws out from our deepest selves a Thank You, and a Yes. (Easter 1980)

"Adoramus te Christe, benedicimus tibi, quia per crucem tuam redemisti mundum."

Adoramus te Christe

"We adore you, Jesus Christ, and we bless your Holy Name; truly your cross and passion bring us life and healing."

Music: Jacques Berthier (1923–1994),
© Ateliers et Presses de Taizé

Reflection Questions

What light does the story of the disciples of Emmaus (Luke 24:13–35) shed on my own journey? Am I sometimes beset by hopelessness or pessimism? Have I ever looked back on my difficulties and discovered that Christ was with me without my realizing it? How can I place the Good News of the Resurrection at the center of my life of faith?

9
A Mystery of Communion

From where could we draw an abundant inner life if the spirit of joy were to disappear from the Church, that unique communion which is the Body of Christ?

What if we were to lose childlike trust in the Eucharist and in the Word of God?

If the common prayer of Christians began to express itself in a language exuding boredom, it would disappoint our expectations and perhaps even frighten people away. Common prayer becomes welcoming when it leaves room for the beauty of singing, for poetry, for the adorable presence of the Risen Lord. (ST)

*W*hile still a child, Brother Roger was confronted with the shocking reality of the divisions wounding the Church. Dissension within a parish, rivalry between parishes, separations between different Protestant denominations and between Protestants and Catholics. But he was also exposed as a child to the beauty of the Orthodox liturgy, and, pastor's son though he was, when the time came for him to leave and continue his studies, lodging was arranged for him with a Catholic widow. Why? She was in great need of extra income to raise her children. Thus, through his parents (whose motives he was aware of), he learned that the love of Christ recognizes no denominational boundaries. A lesson in how to live an authentic Gospel life.

Very soon, his feeling for harmony and his sensitivity made him acutely aware of the discrepancy between calling oneself a Christian and allowing Church divisions to be taken for granted. Later on, confronted with mounting skepticism and disbelief, he understood how serious was the counter-testimony resulting from the splintering of Christians into so many different denominations.

He was often heard quoting these words: "Christ did not come upon the earth to start a new religion, but to offer to every human being communion with God." His first instinct was for the vast potential of community witness: it sprang from the wounds opened by the wars between Christians in Europe, as an antidote to the continuing mistrust about man's humanity and the mission of churches incapable of curbing such deadly impulses.

How overjoyed he was, then, to welcome to Taizé important Church leaders anxious to move forward toward unity: Pope John Paul II;

the primates of the Anglican Church, Michael Ramsey, George Carey, and Rowan Williams, archbishops of Canterbury; fourteen Lutheran bishops from Sweden who came all together; and the Secretary-General of the World Council of Churches, Eugene Carson Blake.

A Ministry of Communion

At the time of Taizé's founding, gathering around the brothers was a group called the Great Community. They were people of fervor who came to seek renewal, attracted by the gospel radicalism of life at Taizé and the freshness in the Protestant world of this kind of liturgical prayer, as well as by its beauty. To live a *"parable of community"* (ST) is to believe it can have sign-value and foster trust in the *"community of communities"* (UP) which is the Church. It also leads people into the mystery of the community of the Trinity, as Christ invited us on the eve of his death: "That they may all be one, as you, Father, are in me and I in you, so that the world may believe" (John 17:21).

When he welcomed Pope John Paul II to Taizé on October 5, 1986, Brother Roger said:

> *With my brothers, our daily hope is for each young person to discover Christ: not simply Christ in isolation, but the "Christ of communion" fully present in the mystery of communion which is his Body, the Church.... This is like a fire burning within us. We would go to*

*the ends of the earth to find ways to make this
possible; we would ask, implore, even beg if
necessary, but never from the outside, always
remaining within that unique communion
which is the Church.*

Do we truly wish to encounter the *"Christ of
communion"*?

Then we must resist various temptations.
For example, the temptation of "coziness," of
community life lived for its own sake only, as
an end in itself, a reassuring space in which we
seek perfection in a beautiful liturgy, at the risk
of neglecting service to the human community.
There is the temptation of a kind of sectarian-
ism, to create a movement which lures us away
from our own church of origin or our parish,
which we begin to criticize from outside. Taizé
sends everyone back to their spiritual family of
origin. Wanting to be *"servants of communion"*
requires us not to compromise, but genuinely
to feel ourselves participants in the whole Body
of Christ. Realistically, we must allow for its
frailness and put up with its weaknesses and
divisions; but then we also share in its treasures
of holiness.

To go forward and better to understand
others, Brother Roger always initiated meetings, going to Rome, to Constantinople, even
to Moscow. With Pope John XXIII he experienced a deep accord which gave him a new
understanding of the ministry of communion

for the universal Church which the Bishop of Rome was called to exercise.

There still remained this anxiety for the Prior of Taizé: what was the place within the Church for this community of brothers from so many different Christian backgrounds? Each one owed his faith in Christ to the Church in which he had been baptized and from which he had received the Word of life. What communion was possible without repudiating these origins? Often he calmed his anxiety by recalling this response, and the spirit beyond the words:

> *"The Church consists of a series of ever-wider concentric circles," said John XXIII. He did not specify in which of them he saw us. But we understood that in the situation in which we found ourselves, we need not worry, we were part of the Church.* (DSF)

He continued to reflect on this question. Twenty years later, during a European Meeting, he said publicly to Pope John Paul II in St. Peter's Basilica:

> *Touched by the witness of my grandmother's life, while still very young I found my own identity as a Christian by reconciling within myself the faith of my origin with the mystery of the Catholic faith without breaking communion with anyone.* (CL)

Such is the generosity and broadmindedness of the communion offered by Christ. Thus it was possible for Brother Roger to receive communion from the hands of the future Pope Benedict XVI during Pope John Paul II's funeral at Rome. He used to receive the Eucharist every day at Taizé, but on this occasion there were cameras present, and so one saw an old man, all hunched over, shrunken, reaching out for the Presence, absorbed in it, given over to it. *"Christ offers himself in the Eucharist. Adorable presence, he is there for those who are poor and helpless"* (ST). Several years earlier he had written:

> *These days I often find myself in the little Romanesque church, near the reserved Eucharist. This place is inhabited by a living Presence: the faith of the Catholic Church has testified to it since the first centuries.* (F)

While the celebration of the Eucharist remains a stumbling block between the churches, in 1970 at Constantinople Patriarch Athenagoras pointed the way, sharing this conviction with Brother Roger: *"The cup and the breaking of bread. There is no other solution; remember!"* (LND). Without waiting for communion among Christians to be fully worked out, we can open ourselves to the Eucharistic transformation, the work of the Spirit.

> *Vast numbers of people have a desire for reconciliation that touches the very depths of their soul. They aspire to this inexhaustible joy: one love, one heart, one and the same communion.*

Holy Spirit, come and place in our hearts the desire to move forward towards a communion; you are the one who leads us to it. (L 2004)

"Veni Sancte Spiritus, tui amoris ignem accende."

"Holy Spirit, come to us. Kindle in us the fire of your love. Holy Spirit, come to us. Holy Spirit, come to us."

Music: Jacques Berthier (1923–1994),
© Ateliers et Presses de Taizé

Reflection Questions

In what way is the Church, the community of believers, significant for my faith-journey? Does it offer an alternative to the individualism so rampant in our society? How can our local Christian communities become places of hospitality for all? What can we do to create understanding among believers of different origins? What role does the Eucharist, the sacrament of communion, play in my spiritual life?

10
Struggle and Contemplation

From now on, in prayer or in struggle, only one thing is disastrous, the loss of love.
Without love, what is the good of believing, or even of giving your body to the flames?
Do you see?
Contemplation and struggle arise from the very same source, Christ who is love.
If you pray, it is out of love.
If you struggle to restore dignity to the exploited, that too is for love.
Will you agree to set out on this road?
At the risk of losing your life for love, will you live Christ for others? (LND)

*T*he love of God, or love of human beings? What is love worth which is never tested? In our churches, as in the whole of society, trends occur regularly like the swings of a pendulum, sometimes with disastrous effects. Now emphasis is placed on concrete action, now on the urgency of prayer, when in fact each of these actions is barren without the other.

To pray: it was the intuitive awareness of the power of this hidden way of working on the world's behalf that led so many young people to gather around the contemplative community on the hill of Taizé in the wake of the Second Vatican Council, and following the tumultuous days of May 1968.

Their consciousness had become global. Voices from Latin America called for revolution, demanding agrarian reforms and denouncing unjust structures of the world economy. The newfound independence of African nations fashioned a new way of thinking about the developing countries of the Southern Hemisphere. People passed along information about the methods of this or that multinational corporation. A kind of peace-at-any-price philosophy sometimes motivated conscientious objection and was found side-by-side with authentically non-violent positions.

In their generous involvement on behalf of the poorest of the poor, Christians sometimes ran the risk of ideology, acting in the name of a few well-chosen Beatitudes turned into a simplistic program for overturning current values. The necessary key had to be rediscovered: seeing human beings through Christ's eyes, their mystery, their divine calling. If activism posed a threat to the gospel energy of some, at Taizé many sensed that Christ's Passover called them to something different: "Struggle and contemplation in order to

become people of communion." This was the rec-
ognizable influence of Brother Roger: *"Nothing is
more responsible than praying"* (PSH).

The Happiness of Free People

For disciples of Jesus, it is urgent not to
get sidetracked into a meaningless opposition
between involvement with people and the inner
life (which itself knows struggles and crises).
"Becoming signs of contradiction in accor-
dance with the Gospel leads us at the same time
to be tireless seekers of communion. This communion is not a refusal of crises or confronta-
tion; it always involves a new birth. It unites us
first of all to those who are oppressed." Such
were the opening words of the intercontinental
team which spoke at Taizé during the meeting
on Easter 1973, tolling the death knell of any
struggle "against" others. The call to an authentic radicalism rooted in the Gospel cannot be
cut off from its source. Brother Roger picked up
the theme the next day:

> *Struggle and contemplation: will we be led
> to situate our existence between these two
> poles?... In the long run, contemplation gives
> rise to happiness. And this happiness of free
> people is the driving-force for our struggle for
> and with all people. It is courage; it is energy
> for taking risks.* (SC)

Witnessing to this is the influence of so many men and women who remain steadfast in the tension between these two realities which, far from being antithetical, actually nourish one another.

To withstand anxieties or skepticism, it is invigorating to be reminded by the holy history of the world — that is, a history which has a meaning — of the biblical reality of the "saving remnant" which always went forward by trusting, not in easy complacency.

> *Never forget that during the most difficult times, very often a small number of women, men, young people, and even children, spread across the earth, have been able to reverse the course of certain historical evolutions.... They can be recognized, they have been shaped by times of unimaginable trials. Through thick and thin, they kept going in the face of overpowering obstacles.* (ST)

Brother Roger knew what he was talking about, both because he and his community were sometimes seriously criticized and rejected, and because they themselves sought contact with witnesses to faith from all corners of the world. There are decisions whose consequences go far beyond what we can understand. For a disciple there is no other way than that of Christ, who took "resolutely" the road to Jerusalem (Luke 9:51). Inevitable difficulties, contradictions, even persecutions can be faced with equanimity only with Christ, in him, for love's sake.

We need only open ourselves to contemplation. It will teach us how to see, and expand the space before us where we will encounter the newness of the Spirit. There is no room here for frenetic activism or for giving up. Neither simplistic denunciation nor an invitation to wage war, Brother Roger's intuition from the 1970s remains a summary of the whole Christian life, where inner life and human solidarity link up in a paradoxical equilibrium, struggle and contemplation, which invite us to the threshold of the mystery: agreeing to become fully human, on a journey of sharing with the most impoverished, because we are filled with a presence of communion.

A Struggle to Love

Struggle then takes the shape of an absolute trust in God's promise of faithfulness by which he stands up for our humanity. He is on our side because he has promised us: "Remember, I am with you always, to the end of the age" (Matthew 28:20). But it is by passing through the cross that our course of action is verified.

> *Peace begins in oneself. But how can we love those who oppress the weak and the poor? And harder still: how can we love our opponent when he claims to be acting in Christ's name? God moves us to pray even for those who hate. God is wounded with the innocent.* (DSF)

Then we understand that the witness expected of us is not first of all that of action or of perfection, but of consenting to our own weaknesses, of mercy toward others, and of our participation in the sufferings of the world, because compassion goes hand in hand with mercy. Such is the *"violence of the peacemakers"*: using the weapons of the Spirit, a struggle to become more human, to have our sensibility heightened by the Gospel and our intelligence purified.

The keyword of these new relations is "reconciliation." Reconciliation within ourselves, reconciliation with the world, and with other people. A reconciliation begun by Christ, a reconciliation of which the Church becomes the instrument when, in the ministry of forgiveness, she offers the opportunity to express repentance of heart and receive the welcome of the Father.

God of peace, although we may be fragile,
we are eager to follow you along the way
that leads us to love as you love us. (PSH)

"El alma que anda en amor; ni cansa, ni se cansa."

"Whoever walks in God's love tires no-one, nor grows weary" (…). (John of the Cross)

Music: Taizé, © Ateliers et Presses de Taizé

Reflection Questions

What kinds of struggle for a more authentic existence are important for me? Are there situations of injustice I feel called upon to try and change? What shape does my inner struggle to be faithful to Christ take? How do prayer and silence help me in these outer and inner combats? Is it possible to "struggle with a reconciled heart"?

11
Kindness of Heart

Whoever lives a life rooted in God chooses to love.

And a heart resolved to love can radiate goodness without limits.

Life is filled with serene beauty for whoever strives to love with trust.

All who choose to love and to say it with their life are led to ask themselves one of the most compelling questions of all: how can we ease the pain and the torment of others, whether they are close at hand or far away?

But what does it mean to love?

Could it be to share the suffering of the most ill-treated? Yes, that's it.

Could it mean having infinite kind-heartedness and forgetting oneself for others, selflessly? Yes, certainly.

And again: what does it mean to love? Loving means forgiving, living as people who are reconciled. And reconciliation always brings a springtime to the soul. (UL)

*I*n his earliest writings, Brother Roger depicted a community of intellectuals open to every concern of the contemporary world. It is clear that he was interested in current ideas, but he gradually came to fear that a certain intellectualism would be satisfied with barren discussions unaccompanied by true openness of heart.

> *Our rational faculty is impaired; it has become impossible to restore its true aspect which is to search for truth in love.* (LTG)

Brother Roger had a bitter experience of this during ecumenical meetings and in his contacts with Church authorities, be they Protestant, Catholic, or Orthodox. He was so desirous of moving forward, yet things always seemed to end up at a standstill, with all sides seeking to justify their own heritage. Thus he suggested: *"Understand with the heart, the mind will catch up later"* (LND).

The Church is *"humble when its own members, far from judging it in bitterness and arrogance, instead consent to love it to the point of giving their own lives in the ongoing attempt to renew its institutions"* (LTG).

What is true for institutions is also true for individuals. During the Second Vatican Council, benefiting from his status (along with Brother Max) as a non-Catholic observer, Brother Roger had the opportunity for many meetings, especially with bishops and theologians from around the world, whom he invited to the community's table. Praying the daily office together, sharing a simple meal: such exchanges encouraged openness to other people, to other cultures, to a greater love of the entire Church. Hearts were opened more and more.

Allowing Christ to Transfigure the Shadows Themselves

With keen watchfulness, Brother Roger was quick to encourage and support even the smallest gesture toward fulfilling the requirements of the Gospel. But always, with his constant dread of scandalizing anyone, he kept silent and refused to criticize this person or that Church initiative:

> *Communion is one of the most beautiful names of the Church. In it there can be no severity towards one another, but only transparency, heartfelt kindness, compassion.* (CL)

Kindheartedness: his mother had been the image of it for him. He experienced kindheartedness in Pope John XXIII and also in Dom Helder Camara, in Bishop Wojtyla, the future Pope John Paul II, and in Mother Teresa of Calcutta, with whom he forged true bonds of friendship, and in many, many others, men and women of deep inner lives. Through faith such power for good is accessible to each and every one of us.

> *Christ offers us all we need to go to the well-springs, the Gospel, the Eucharist, the peace of forgiveness ... and Christ's holiness is no longer something unattainable; it is here, close at hand. It overflows above all in an inexhaustible goodness of the human heart, in a selfless love.* (F)

"Just as you did it to one of the least of these who are members of my family ..." (Matthew 25:40). The call of Christ is unequivocal. He can be recognized in every person who suffers. Like Saint John of the Cross, Brother Roger often repeated:

> *In the evening of our life we shall be judged by our love, by the kindness which we have allowed little by little to grow within us and to blossom in compassion toward every human being.* (LTG)

Moved by what he heard from Latin American bishops, and as someone always concerned to act, Brother Roger set up Operation Hope to foster sharing between North and South, East and West. At the time of Mother Teresa's death he recalled:

> *We had this conviction in common: a communion in God stimulates us to alleviate human*

suffering on earth. Yes, when we soothe the trials of others, we encounter Christ. (GH)

He could not forget the insistence with which one of the sisters in Calcutta entrusted to him an undersized and sickly baby girl only a few months old. "In France, she may survive!" It was utterly unrealistic. But Brother Roger assented, and the infant, Marie-Sonaly, lived.

But easing the suffering of others does not always require a great deal. A look, increased attentiveness, a sensitive gesture, a way of being [ ] … *"Only compassion allows us to see others as they are. When we look at them with love, we discern in each person the profound beauty of the human soul"* (GH). Going personally to stay in such places of misery as the China Sea, and Haiti, and a shantytown in Nairobi, to an earthquake-stricken town in Southern Italy, to celebrate Christmas in a woman's prison in Chile: in all these Brother Roger allowed himself to enter into human situations of profound dereliction.

In doing so, he experienced an entirely different way of being present to others. Recognizing our inability to change things in any conclusive way in a complex world, rather than causing us to despair, can liberate in us new energies of compassion. Heartfelt kindness doesn't give up; instead it gets us going. Who will we go to meet?

Making Our Homes a House of Nazareth

In a modern version of the exhortation of Athanasius, a saint of the Egyptian Church, the Letter from Haiti invites everyone, without needing to traipse all over the world, to make their own home *"a place of compassion amidst human beings, a little Church community."* This was the atmosphere that the Taizé community sought to recreate in its manner of welcoming people.

Thus, at Easter 2000, the philosopher Paul Ricoeur wrote that he came to Taizé "to confirm in some way … that however radical evil may be, it is not as deep as goodness." He continued, "I see outpourings of kindness in the community among the brothers in their tranquil and unassuming hospitality, and in the prayer, where thousands of young people who have no way to articulate their understanding of good and evil, of God, of grace, of Jesus Christ, have nonetheless a fundamental inclination towards the good." At its root is Christ's gaze, full of kindness for each one of us. He alone can move us, and liberate us from ourselves.

Thirty years earlier, at Easter 1970, an intercontinental team announcing with Brother Roger the creation of a Council of Youth expressed how much the Eucharist, entrusted to the Church by Christ, by making our hearts more inclusive, transforms the world and makes kindness circulate.

"As we journey across the desert towards a Church of sharing, the Eucharist gives us the courage not to hoard the manna, to refuse to stockpile worldly possessions, and to share not only the bread of life, but also the goods of this earth." To be motivated by a love which requires more than mere words, we need to know where our hearts find rest.

God of all human beings, you invite each one of us to be a reflection of your presence. By the Holy Spirit you have inscribed in each of us the will of your love, not on tablets of stone but in the depths of our soul. And, by the peace of our hearts, you enable us to make life beautiful for those around us. (SHG)

"Ubi caritas et amor, ubi caritas, Deus ibi est."

Ubi caritas

U - bi ca - ri - tas   et a - mor,   u - bi ca - ri - tas   De-us i - bi est.

"Where there is charity and love, God is there."

Music: Jacques Berthier (1923–1994),
© Ateliers et Presses de Taizé

Reflection Questions

What does it mean to "understand with the heart"? What examples of kindheartedness have I encountered in the course of my life? What acts of kindness have I been able to accomplish? Where do I find the strength for this? What do these words of Brother Roger mean to me: *"Only compassion allows us to see others as they are."*

12
Each of Us Has
a Pastoral Gift

*To love Christ is to receive from him, imme-
diately, a greater or lesser share in a pastoral
gift. God entrusts to everybody one or more
other persons. This pastoral gift, however
small, is a source from which to draw the
inspiration to communicate Christ. It allows
each one to accomplish his pilgrimage in the
whole human family.* (DSF)

*T*he young man who first formulated
what would be his lifelong project in
1941 was inspired by the Benedictine motto:
"*Ora et labora*," Pray and Work, but he transformed it by also expressing its aim: "*ut regnet*,"
that Christ shall reign. While prayer and work
are prescribed to hasten the coming of the
Kingdom, the evolving community would also
be concerned with the problems of the world
and search for ways of being present to it. Of
letting their light shine out.

This recalls the "Little Source" of the Taizé Community, which expresses *"the essential which makes a common life possible."* In it one finds *"'I am'.... but also 'you are the light of the world'"* (ST). Christ invites us to share in the mission he received from his Father by entrusting us to one another.

> *When we realize that God loves even the most forsaken human being, then our hearts open to others. We are made more aware of the dignity of each person and we ask ourselves: how can we help prepare a different future?... Faith becomes credible and is passed on above all when it is lived out.* (GH)

Like a Birth of the Kingdom Within

In his own ministry, Brother Roger sought above all the meeting of souls. Was he reserved, shy, fearful of crowds? Yes, but that was not the important thing. How did he perceive his personal ministry? Through listening, he could communicate Christ. *"Listening to others fosters in them a kind of ongoing birth of the kingdom within"* (HT). Whether watching intently or with eyes closed, his total absorption in an inner communication was evident beyond any words.

Those to whom he listened were struck by the intensity of such attention — simple, prayerful, compassionate and full of mercy. And of blessing as well. Very often those who came to him were unable to understand his whispered responses. There might even be long times of silence. Comfort came from Another.

To be present in this way demands self-surrender. To be wholly available to another person, to allow oneself to be enthralled by him or her. To permit oneself to be touched in this way by someone else is no superficial affair; it does not leave the listener unscathed. Over a long time, might this lead to a kind of weariness? That would proceed from a sense of being "above," with an accompanying risk of condescension. It must never be forgotten that such listening is, first of all, recognition of the other, a search to uncover in him or her the outlines of Christ's face.

Brother Roger found here a never-ending source of inspiration to hasten the coming of the Kingdom. He sought to *"fully understand the other."* In doing so, *"it often happens that the one who listens to another is himself led to the essential, and the other never even suspects it"* (DSF). It was thus that he was able to glimpse the deepest aspirations of his time.

Understanding What Lies Beneath Another's Heart

"Like each and every one of us, Jesus needed to hear a human voice saying: 'You know that I love you' " (DSF). What would we, like Peter, answer him in our turn? (John 21:15). Would we rec-

ognize him today in the many men, women, young people, children or the elderly who suffer cruelly from loneliness, from the lack of a compassionate listener? In a joint statement, Mother Teresa and Brother Roger spoke about the Western phenomenon of "invisible homes for the dying." But there is also a danger in oversimplified psychologizing.

> *Often we know little of the context in which the life of those who confide in us is unfolding. That is not the important thing. In any case, to answer them with advice or by categorical "you musts" would lead them astray. Listen to them in order to clear the ground and to prepare in them the ways of Christ.* (DSF)

It is not only a matter of giving people the opportunity to unburden what weighs on their hearts or makes them suffer, but also of helping them discover how to find a way out of these interior prisons, of awakening each one to the intimate presence of the Spirit of Christ. *"Already, in him, we are healed by one another"* (LND).

With the influx of participants in international meetings and year-round visitors to Taizé, the community discovered its vocation of hospitality and listening. Brother Roger began to ask other brothers also to make themselves available at the end of the prayer. But always they should be careful to remain *"men who listen, never 'spiritual masters.' Those who set themselves up as masters can easily get caught up in a spiritual pretension which is the death of the soul."*

One has only to read Brother Roger to understand that he never hesitated to share his own past spiritual experiences, humbly, and without ever wishing to teach a lesson. He was well aware of his own contradictions and weakness. Underlining a possible temptation for him, for the Taizé Community, for us all, he wrote:

> *Yes, refuse to monopolize anyone at all for oneself. The Virgin Mary shows us a gesture of offering: she did not keep her Son for herself, she offered him to the world.* (DSF)

Purity of intention and letting go of possessiveness: there is no other way.

Each evening there is now a time when anyone can meet with a brother in the church, or request the sacrament of reconciliation from a priest. Yet this time for listening is simply a sign of how all Christians are invited to live with those whom God has placed in their lives and entrusted to them: to open a spiritual dialogue, *"until even in a life harrowed by tribulations he can perceive God's hope, or at least human hope"* (DSF).

A Mystical Vision of the Human Being

Becoming inwardly attentive to even infinitesimal growth, we sometimes sense that we are encountering another human being in all his or her mystery, as one *"in whom both weakness*

and radiance dwells, the abyss and fullness" (LF).
Between word and silence is revealed *"the special gift of God in a person, the pivot of their existence"* (LND).

Then, wishing to embrace the plan of God for that person, a great desire arises in us: *"If, when they left, the young would have discovered the gift placed within them.... If they in turn had the burning desire to make straight for others the ways of Christ..."* (DSF).

We find ourselves radically caught up in a solidarity greater than ourselves. From then on we hear the call to respond to our brothers and sisters.

> *When the tempter whispers in our ear his 'what's the use?' and makes us slip and fall to the roadside, there is always a friend to take us by the hand and pull us up. And in our turn, if one day he slips, we will pull him out of the rut.* (DSF)

But what happens when we come up against lack of understanding, and the other seems to refuse a mutual listening? There is the risk of reducing such people simply to their ideas, no longer recognizing them as human beings. Since the Taizé Community has always eluded conventional categories, Brother Roger found himself up against serious criticism as much from French Protestant institutions as from the Catholic Church.

One day, when he was summoned to Rome by the Holy Office, he wrote: *"Try to understand those who oppose and perhaps one day, unexpectedly, a person-to-person talk will take place and everything will suddenly become clear"* (LND). Such an attitude reveals the consistency of a life. The light of a life!

> *Jesus, peace for our hearts, your Gospel comes to open our eyes to the fullness of your love: it is forgiveness, inner light.* (PSH)

"Christe, lux mundi, qui sequitur te habebit lumen vitae, lumen vitae."

Christe, lux mundi

"Christ, you are light for those who follow you. You come to bring to all the light of life."

Music: Taizé, © Ateliers et Presses de Taizé

Reflection Questions

What enables us to discover the gifts that God has placed in us? How can I put the gifts I have received at the service of others? What is needed to be a good listener? Can I accept the fact that other people do not correspond to the image I have of them or my expectations for them? Is it still possible to journey together?

13
A Passionate Waiting

Prayer is both struggle and surrender. Prayer is also waiting, waiting for the walls of our inner resistance to break down. In the same way, Christ in his earthly life knew times of intense patience....

There are people who almost never experience any detectable resonance of a presence in them. They are in waiting their whole life long, and that is the fire behind their seeking. For them contemplation is a struggle, it does not bring immediate fullness flooding over them, it does not arouse any spontaneous outburst of feeling for Christ. (LND)

L inking prayer to the fervent waiting which fuels the urgent call of the Apocalypse, "Come, Lord Jesus!" (Revelation 22:20) to rise in us and echo indefinitely, Brother Roger invites us to make use of the *"spiritual capacity"* placed within us by the Spirit. It makes us fully alive, beings of longing and of commitment.

This call, which is not only eschatological waiting nor a simple cry for help for ourselves or another person, is intercession, a waiting which keeps us alert and widens our outlook to the utmost. *"Ut regnet"*: that He may reign! In every person, on every matter....

Nothing is insignificant any longer.

> *Throughout our days and our nights, there are actions which we perform for Christ's sake, and these actions become prayer: forgiveness, reconciliation, the struggle to remain faithful in marriage or in celibacy consecrated to God. Such signs, and many others, are a language by which we speak to Christ. Performed for him, they show him our love.* (F)

We are longing for love, and a purification by means of which we no longer center on ourselves. *"His love is a fire."* What does it matter that we have very few words to pray with, or that our waiting sometimes seems disappointing! We learn in this way a kind of passivity and patience.

There is Another in each one of us who prays and who struggles, who enables us to resist all the fears which paralyze us, all the soul-searching which impedes our inner life when faced with the desire for tangible experiences. That Other allows us to identify and *"let go of bad sorrow"* (GLA). And at last to hear again these words: *"Do not forget that God takes care of all your cares"* (ST).

Sing Christ's Praises Until
You Are Joyful and Serene

Our hearts, *"suspended in the utter silence of God"* (HT), can easily become a battlefield at times. Far from the state of responsiveness that we seek, we may be assaulted by images and thoughts that seem to distract us from prayer.... The temptation then is to call upon all our energies and by sheer hard work to devise an artificial concentration or silence. *"In a life of communion with God, nothing can be forced, to the point where sometimes the more we try, the less we succeed"* (HT).

Do not dwell on difficulties or darkness. Without self-indulgence or colluding with the Tempter, go on your way, singing.

> *When I was still very young, I was struck by these words going back several centuries before Christ: "Praised be God who has delivered me from the enemy!" The spirit of praise takes us out of ourselves in order to hand over to God whatever may worry or torment us. And our deepest resistances are transfigured.* (PSH)

Brother Roger, so imaginative and perceptive, knew that a person's inner equilibrium is often shaken. Return to the road with confidence: God can kindle a fire from any kind of wood. Far from trotting out all sorts of guilt-inducing advice about using one's will-power, he resolutely affirmed his trust: *"To those who are surprised to find themselves saying, 'My thoughts wander, my heart is scattered,' the Gospel replies: 'God is greater than your heart'"* (HT). In recognizing this inner Guest, the dignity of every person is revealed, his or her own deep dynamic, while trust sprouts and works its healing.

> *Handing over to God our worries, our resistances, liberates energies enabling us to see beyond situations, even beyond individuals. Perhaps it is in this way that we already possess a piece of eternity?* (FSF)

"Do Not Look Upon My Sins, but on the Faith of Your Church"

Drawing upon the witness of the communion of saints to emerge from a period of deep doubt, the young Roger said to himself: *"Rely on those you trust, whom you know to be of great honesty"* (CL). But his whole life long he grappled with doubt, which made him very much a sharer in the questioning of so many of his contemporaries, assailed by feelings of unworthiness, vague guilt, or anxious skepticism. Surreptitiously fear would creep in to undermine his trust in himself.

> *How can we keep going? By daring to move forward after every discouragement, after every failure. Not with an ideal heart, but*

*with the one we have. Not with the heart we
don't have: God will change it.* (DSF)

Between doubt and faith the line of separation is so tenuous that the two often coexist in
us. And that is where a spiritual battle can take
place, like a clash between death-dealing pow-
ers and the Spirit of the Risen Lord. Whoever
walks in the footsteps of Jesus cannot avoid this
struggle, where the stakes are much larger than
ourselves. Waiting becomes passion, a suffering with Christ. In 1978, in the cathedral of
what was still then Leningrad, Brother Roger
spoke to seminarians:

> *The more you walk with Christ, the more
> you will be led on to the mountain of temp-
> tation. He himself was there. The closer we
> draw, invisibly, to the agony of Christ, the
> more we bear in ourselves a reflection of the
> Risen Lord.* (DSF)

With Christ, the light of Easter!

Waiting for communion also compels us
to take up arms against the "Divider," the one
who encourages us to take divisions for granted.
Faithful to his own call, faithful to the Gospel,
Brother Roger opened a prophetic channel
within the Church, without any institutional
recognition. In Scripture one sees that prophets
expose themselves to mockery. But he could
not resist the Spirit. Anxious to be part of the

continuity of God's covenant with his people, to call to conversion and to open new pathways of life, he was willing to take risks.

Brother Roger confided, at a time when he saw the ecumenical wave which had aroused so many hopes at the time of the Second Vatican Council beginning to collapse:

> *I am filled with a conviction: this great struggle we have to wage comes up against the powers of the world of darkness. They do not want visible unity. They know that Christ is in an agony of suffering confronted with his Church torn to bits. And so I have accepted that the struggle may become even harder.* (VP)

Brother Roger here gives us a key to his inner life: with Christ, to accept reality, the reality of the seed cast into the earth, of the vine that is pruned.... In this Easter dynamic, the Gospel's call to reconciliation right away (Matthew 5:23–24) still remains to be heard. Shall we enter into this prayerful waiting and take an active part in a visible communion within the Church?

> *Holy Spirit, even when our words are almost unable to express our longing for communion with you, your invisible presence dwells within each one and so a joy may be offered to us.* (PSH)

"Mon âme se repose en paix sur Dieu seul :
de lui vient mon salut. Oui, sur Dieu seul mon
âme se repose, se repose en paix."

Mon âme se repose

*"In God alone my soul can find rest and peace,
in God my peace and joy. Only in God my soul
can find its rest, find its rest and peace."*

Music: Jacques Berthier (1923–1994),
© Ateliers et Presses de Taizé

Reflection Questions

Have there been times in my life when I felt
God was far away? How did I deal with this?
What enabled me to keep going? What do these
words mean to me: "If our hearts condemn us,
God is greater than our hearts" (1 John 3:20)?
Have I ever realized that God is present for me
beyond my doubts and my feelings of empti-
ness? What does this mean for the way I pray?

14
A Wider Outlook

Christians today are living at a time when the vocation to universality, to ecumenicity, to catholicity, placed within them by the Gospel, can find unprecedented fulfillment....

Will their hearts be big enough, their imaginations open enough, their love afire enough to respond to one of the main calls of the Gospel: to take the risk of reconciling themselves in every new day, and in this way to be a leaven of confident trust between nations and races, in the dough of the human family which, in order to survive, is aspiring to unity throughout the world? (HT)

*T*he communion to which Christ calls us goes beyond the world of the Church and cannot help but make us sensitive to the sufferings of the whole human family. Sharing the Eucharist, or praying together in front of the reserved Sacrament, transforms our way of looking and allows us to *"discover in the person in front of us Christ made man"* (UP). Unsuspected connections appear. An inner spirit surges up far beyond mere conformity, and the radiance of a reconciled humanity appears.

> *God loves me — this reality sometimes seems almost beyond our reach. But the day of a discovery can dawn: when I let myself be touched by God's love, my life opens up to others.* (L2000)

This experience turns our life upside down, and reveals the urgency of opening our hearts, the importance of the "sacrament of brotherhood."

Leaving Switzerland for France, Brother Roger sought to settle on some fault-line of the world. In ultimately choosing Taizé, he opted for a place of poverty, scarred by neglect. By maintaining contacts with a network of the Resistance in Lyon and by sheltering Jews and other fugitives who had to remain hidden, he took his share of risk in order to help others.

At the end of the war, concern for the defeated, former enemies, German prisoners confined in nearby camps and sometimes mistreated, led him and his brothers to a new experience of compassion. Since that time there has scarcely been a conflict on the planet which has not had an audible echo at Taizé. *"The person who prays has a guiding star. Like a hidden, invisible pole, it draws him on…. He becomes another person for other people"* (LND).

Firmly Situated Within the Wounds of the Human Family

One characteristic of the Taizé Community from its beginning has been its desire to be involved in the life of the wider world. It has continuously kept in contact with activists from many movements concerned with social justice, as is shown by the various testimonies which prefaced Brother Roger's *Introduction to Community Life,* published in 1944.

With the return of peace, France found itself "mission territory," and the French Church wrestled with ways to reconnect with the working classes. They experimented using the example of priest-workers: some brothers of Taizé lived this kind of commitment in small groups in Montceau-les-Mines and Marseille, discovering both its value and its difficulty. Other brothers were then sent to places of great poverty in countries of both the South and the North. Some of these small "fraternities" were temporary, attached to a specific project or mission. Others have proved longer-lasting, such as those in Brazil, Bangladesh, Seoul, and Dakar.

Current events, to the extent that we are attentive to them and ready and willing to respond, constantly offer such opportunities. Mindful of the suffering and isolation of Christians behind the Iron Curtain, some brothers traveled to meet with them. Sometimes Brother Roger went also. Some brothers learned Russian. Any time it was possible to take part in a church camp, go on a pilgrimage such as at Czestochowa, or help at a construction site, some young people were sent to do so.

Strategies were found to invite young Hungarians, Czechs, Poles, etc., who then met one another at Taizé. Exchanges became possible. There were times when Europe quietly "breathed with both lungs," in the words of Pope John Paul II. Witnessing to faith could not be confined by borders.

"The body of Christ, His Church, must always be expanding to the scale of the universe" (SC). It is impossible not to hear in these words an echo of the prophet Isaiah: "For your Maker is your husband.... The God of the whole earth he is called" (Isaiah 54:2–5). Isaiah is inviting Jerusalem to anticipate the joy of her universal motherhood, to make her tent larger in order to welcome all of her promised posterity. "All your children shall be disciples of the Lord." It is an invitation to fruitfulness, to a future of justice. Such is the ultimate horizon.

But today, as Christians, there are personal decisions that need to be made if we are to be faithful to the Covenant into which our baptism entered us. Here we confront alternatives:

> *Either, in the image of a humanity exploding into innumerable fragments, the People of God too will remain splintered into multitudes of opposing parts, indifferent to each other, incapable of sharing the joys and the sufferings of the whole human family. Or else, Christians*

are going to be reconciled, and widen their solidarity to include all human beings. The Church will become what she is, the seed of a new humanity, reconciled at last. (DSF)

A genuine catholicity cannot be denominational, or subject to majority rule. God is always on the side of those who weep. Consequently, during the Second Vatican Council, Brother Roger, before rejoicing over the adoption of a text he favored, which was however not unanimously passed, requested a prayer for the minority who felt unrecognized. It comes about that in opening itself to all the misery of the world in daily prayer, morning and evening, the heart becomes wider and is more generous in its intercessions.

God Constantly Offers Us Overflowing Life

Loving the Church in isolation, without Christ, ends in intransigence. But to love Christ alone, without his body, makes us narrow-minded. Loving Christ and loving the Church is one and the same thing, and these words tirelessly challenge me. (F)

All this was already foreshadowed in the first little pamphlet written when he was alone at Taizé in 1941. And yet how often did Brother Roger have to let God lead him where he didn't plan to go! His project was ambitious, because he ardently desired to work for the visible unity of the Church, but it was modest in its human dimensions: *"I said to my first brothers, we will stop at a dozen brothers"* (SC).

He had to change the scale, to widen his outlook without setting limits to God's call. To move from the intimate poetic quality of the little Romanesque church to a concrete structure which at first seemed too massive, but then itself had to be further enlarged, and then even that facade torn down to accommodate still more people. He had to cross oceans, to visit the largest cities of the world. We in our turn find ourselves shaken up and prompted to tear down walls of separation, to avoid all forms of exclusion or division. From now on, one standard of discernment is called for in our lives: the *"sense of the universal"* (LND).

On the day he died, Brother Roger was working on his annual letter, but fatigue prevented him from finishing his sentence: *"To the extent that our community creates possibilities in the human family to broaden ..."* (UL). That last word, "broaden," like the dots of the ellipsis following, forms a kind of last will and testament, an unusual one, but very much in the style of Brother Roger. In the confident trust which he radiated, this incompleteness becomes the very place of his legacy to us.

> *What do you ask of us, Lord Christ? Above all to carry one another's burdens, and to entrust them to you in our prayer, which always remains poor.... When we let ourselves*

*be welcomed by you, the suffering servant,
the inward eye perceives, beyond our own
confusion, a reflection of the Christ of glory,
the Risen Lord.* (DSF)

Laudate omnes gentes, laudate Dominum.
Laudate omnes gentes, laudate Dominum.

Laudate omnes gentes

*"Sing praises, all you peoples! Sing praises to the
Lord!"*

Music: Jacques Berthier (1923–1994),
© Ateliers et Presses de Taizé

Reflection Questions

How can we discover more and more the
universal dimensions of faith in Christ? What
can we do to turn our churches into places
where all feel at home? In what ways can we
reach out to others instead of waiting for them
to come to us? Where are the needs around us
to which we can respond? What kinds of dialogue is it possible to have with those who do
not share our outlook?

15
A Pilgrimage of Trust

If we could always remember that Christ is communion.... He did not come to earth to start one more religion, but to offer to all a communion in God. His disciples are called to be a humble leaven of trust and peace within humanity.

When communion among Christians is a life and not a theory, it radiates hope. Still more, it can help sustain the indispensable search for world peace. How, then, could Christians still remain divided? (GH)

*R*egular visitors to Taizé know there is something new to discover each time they arrive: new faces, living arrangements, songs, suggestions.... Nothing seems frozen in place. And yet, from the very beginning, what a sense of continuity! There is openness and tradition, creativity and faithfulness, a feeling of life....

In 1965, the Second Vatican Council came to an end. As an observer, Brother Roger was delighted with the work accomplished, all the while estimating the difficulties that would be arising from within the Church itself, traditionalists against progressives. He wanted to sustain the momentum of so many people of good will searching for a communion in God.

In publishing *The Dynamic of the Provisional*, respectful of the institutions he encouraged people to accept, he did not try to present spontaneity as sacred, but invited everyone to that radical dispossession which is necessary to live a life following the footsteps of Christ, and deeply anchored in the mystery of the Church: not to settle in, not to hang on.

> *For Christians, life is all beginnings. They stand at the genesis of situations; they are men or women of dawnings, of perpetual discoveries. They keep on waiting when there seems nothing to wait for.* (DSF)

In accepting our place within history, we acknowledge ourselves to be both heirs of the past and people responsible for the future, part of a Church tradition which is spurred on and renewed by the generosity with which we welcome the Holy Spirit. In this way, our capacity today to achieve new things unfurls: *"God condemns no one to immobility. He never closes the ways ahead. God is always offering new ones, even if they are sometimes narrow"* (HT).

Already in the Sixties, Brother Roger sensed the risk of a *"generation gap"* (DP). Through his ministry of listening, he was aware of how disoriented many of the young people who came to Taizé were. Affected by what he had experienced in Rome and searching for something to suggest to them, he hit upon the idea of a Council of Youth. So, boldly, he proposed an international team of young people who, at Easter 1970, would announce the beginning of the preparations. He had no idea where this would lead. But he saw the need to propose acts of hope, and he did so as a tireless discoverer of new paths.

> *I would go to the ends of the earth if necessary, to the farthest reaches of the globe, to speak over and over again of my confidence in the new generations, my confidence in the young.* (LND)

A Nomad Church

Especially attentive to what was brewing in the countries behind the Iron Curtain, Brother Roger encouraged young people:

> *Alone before Christ, you will have the courage to wait for the course of history, even at its most ineluctable, to burst wide open. This hope produces surging creativity, which overthrows all the determinisms of injustice, hatred, and oppression. Alone before Another,*

hope given by him. Hope that invents the world anew. (LND)

In a new relationship with their elders, these young people discovered real responsibilities, and as they did, saw the need to widen their scope. Some learned to love a Church open to a planetary dimension, made up of all races, a Church both poor and excessively rich, committed to increasing justice, divided and suffering, but celebrating in the Risen Christ the manifestation of a love which knows no bounds.

When divisions and rivalries bring things to a standstill, nothing is more important than setting out to visit and listen to one another, and to celebrate the paschal mystery together. (DSF)

In following them we find ourselves invited to changes in our lives, sometimes ones whereby we seem to be standing still, fruits of inner work or of reflection, sometimes ones marked by encounters which open us far beyond anything we had thought we were looking for.

How to imagine, from within the Church, the informal structures needed for a Council of Youth? Mission impossible. So that effort was suspended, but without interrupting the deeper dynamic. Soon a Pilgrimage of Trust on Earth got under way, which still continues after the death of Brother Roger with small and large meetings on all the continents. Such an ability to begin again in trust, without straying off course, is only possible to those who make themselves available to the call of God: "Walk before me!" (Genesis 17:2).

On his first visit to Rome in 1949, to see Pope Pius XII, Brother Roger made the acquaintance of his colleague, Msgr. Montini, the future Pope Paul VI. As a constant reader of St. Augustine, who compared the Christian life to a pilgrimage, he introduced himself and his brothers as *"pilgrims on the road"* (SC). They were following the path of Abraham, of the people of Israel, of Peter, James and John, who had to go down from the mountain of the Transfiguration.

This image never lost its appeal for Brother Roger. It was in Chile that he finished writing the *"Itinerary of a Pilgrim."* Its guideposts for a demanding inner life provide landmarks for discernment, and beckon us to make courageous decisions. It is not so much a matter of leaving home, as of going out of ourselves in order to *"identify ourselves with Christ Jesus, born poor among the poor."*

> *Without looking back, you want to follow Christ: remember that you cannot walk in Christ's steps and at the same time follow yourself. He is the way, and on this way you will be drawn irresistibly to a simple life, a life of sharing.* (DSF)

From One Beginning to Another

Why delay? Christ says over and over to us: "You, follow me" (John 21:22). Why always wait for someone else to take the first step? There is no time to waste! While still very young, Brother Roger already understood this; it was the commitment of his life: *"Begin with yourself ..."* (GH). Yes, let us open ourselves to these ever renewed beginnings, which alone can nourish hope.

> *For trust to arise on earth we need to begin with ourselves, making our way forward with a reconciled heart, living in peace with those around us.... Even if I am empty-handed, can I be a ferment of trust in my own situation, understanding others more and more?* (GH)

Our momentum sometimes slows down. Early enthusiasm can wane; *acedia* (spiritual depression) can threaten. Our expectant waiting can sink into lethargy. If, without allowing ourselves to be discouraged, we set out each day on the journey like the disciples on the way to Emmaus, a surprise awaits us: Christ the pilgrim walks alongside us (Luke 24:13–35).

He is the companion who wishes to speak to our hearts. He illuminates the Scriptures for us, restoring our hope; he sends us back to our brothers and sisters and gives us boldness to shoulder our responsibilities. When he was 80, Brother Roger could write with renewed confidence: *"If, at each dawn, we were able to welcome the new day like*

a beginning of a new life ..." (L1994), and quoting
St. Gregory of Nyssa: *"All who go forward toward
God go from one beginning to another."* Choosing to
live, choosing to love: the promise of a communion. *"Unhoped-for joy!"* (GH).

> *God of all loving, we long to be attentive*
> *when deep within us your call rings out:*
> *"Onward, and may your soul live!"* (PSH)

I am sure I shall see the goodness of the Lord in
the land of the living. Yes, I shall see the goodness of our God, hold firm, trust in the Lord!

Music: Taizé, ©Ateliers et Presses de Taizé

Reflection Questions

Do I see my life as a pilgrimage, a journey? What realities have I been called to leave
behind? Where am I heading? What supports
me on this journey? What can I do when I am
tempted to settle down? Does prayer help my
life to go "from one beginning to another"?

For Further Reading

By Brother Roger

Glimmers of Happiness, GIA Publications 2007

Praying in Silence of Heart, GIA Publications 2007

Peace of Heart in All Things, GIA Publications 2004

About Brother Roger

Choose to Love: Brother Roger of Taizé 1915-2005, Les Presses de Taizé/GIA Publications 2006

DVD: *Meeting Brother Roger of Taizé,* GIA Publications 2006

About Taizé

O. Clément, *A Meaning to Life,* GIA Publications 1997

J. Santos, *A Community Called Taizé,* InterVarsity Press 2009

To learn the songs of Taizé or to visit the Community: www.taize.fr

Also available in the
"15 Days of Prayer" series:

Saint Augustine *(Jaime García)*
978-0-7648-0655-6, paper

Saint Benedict *(André Gozier)*
978-1-56548-304-0, paper

Saint Bernadette of Lourdes *(François Vayne)*
978-1-56548-314-9, paper

Saint Bernard *(Emery Pierre-Yves)*
978-0764-805745, paper

Dietrich Bonhoeffer *(Matthieu Arnold)*
978-1-56548-311-8, paper

Saint Catherine of Siena *(Chantal van der
   Plancke and Andrè Knockaert)*
978-156548-310-1, paper

Pierre Teilhard de Chardin *(André Dupleix)*
978-0764-804908, paper

Saint Vincent de Paul *(Jean-Pierre Renouard)*
978-1-56548-357-6, paper

The Curé of Ars *(Pierre Blanc)*
978-0764-807138, paper

Saint Dominic *(Alain Quilici)*
978-0764-807169, paper

Saint Katharine Drexel *(Leo Luke Marcello)*
978-0764-809231, paper

Don Bosco *(Robert Schiele)*
978-0764-807121, paper

Charles de Foucauld *(Michael Lafon)*
978-0764-804892, paper

Saint Francis de Sales *(Claude Morel)*
978-0764-805752, paper

Saint Francis of Assisi *(Thaddée Matura)*
978-1-56548-315-6, paper

Saint Jeanne Jugan *(Michel Lafon)*
978-1-56548-329-3, paper

Saint Eugene de Mazenod *(Bernard Dullier)*
978-1-56548-320-0, paper

Saint Louis de Montfort *(Veronica Pinardon)*
978-0764-807152, paper

Henri Nouwen *(Robert Waldron)*
978-1-56548-324-8, paper

Saint Martín de Porres: A Saint of the Americas *(Brian J. Pierce)*
978-0764-812163, paper

Meister Eckhart *(André Gozier)*
978-0764-806520, paper

Thomas Merton *(André Gozier)*
978-1-56548-330-9, paper

Saint Elizabeth Ann Seton *(Betty Ann McNeil)*
978-0764-808418, paper

Johannes Tauler *(André Pinet)*
978-0764-806537, paper

Saint Teresa of Ávila *(Jean Abiven)*
978-0764-805738, paper

Saint Thomas Aquinas *(André Pinet)*
978-0764-806568, paper